CW00408120

Welcome to Seville!

This opening fold-out contains a general map of Seville to help you visualise the 6 districts discussed in this guide, and 4 pages of valuable information, handy tips and useful addresses.

Discover Seville through 6 districts and 6 maps

A Catedral / Real Alcázar / Santa Cruz
B Centro
C Arenal / Triana
D Universidad / Parque de María Luisa
E Macarena / Feria
F San Vicente / San Lorenzo / Cartuja

For each district there is a double-page of addresses (restaurants – listed in ascending order of price – cafés, bars, tearooms, music venues and shops), followed by a fold-out map for the relevant area with the essential places to see (indicated on the map by a star ★). These places are by no means all that Seville has to offer, but to us they are unmissable. The grid-referencing system (**A** B2) makes it easy for you to pinpoint addresses quickly on the map.

Transport and hotels in Seville

The last fold-out consists of a transport map and 4 pages of practical information that include a selection of hotels.

Index

In alphabetical order and with a map reference that allows you to pinpoint them quickly on one of the maps, the street names, monuments and places to visit mentioned in this guide.

VIEW OF THE CATHEDRAL

September

Bienal de Arte Flamenco
→ *Even-numbered years*
www.bienalflamenco.org
Performances by the great flamenco artists at venues throughout the city.

Feria Mundial del Flamenco
→ *Odd-numbered years*
International flamenco event bringing together the leading performers of this popular art.

November

**Festival de Sevilla,
Cine y Deporte**
Original festival on the theme of sport in movies.

BUDGET

Restaurants
One tapa: €1.50–2.50.
Lunch: €10–12.
À la carte evening meal:
€15–20.
Note: The à la carte prices given in this guide are for a main course and a dessert. Be aware that in restaurants bread is often charged as extra.

Accommodation
A double room in a *hostal*:
€30–40.

Museums
Entrance fee: €1.50–8.

Out and about
Coffee: €0.80–1.20.
Beer: €2.
Nightclub entrance fee, including a drink: €10–12.

SEVILLE AROUND THE CLOCK

Meal times
Breakfast around 10am; lunch from 2pm; dinner around 9.30–10pm.

Nightlife
Sevillians really only go out on Thursday, Friday and Saturday nights, and they rarely start their rounds of the tapas bars or *copas* (half bar, half nightclub) before midnight. Dancing – *sevillanas*, disco or trance – doesn't really get underway before 2am and goes on until dawn and sometimes into the morning!

Opening hours
Banks
→ *Mon-Fri 8.30am–2pm*
Stores
→ *Mon-Fri 10am–1.30pm, 5–8.30pm; Sat 10.30am–1.30pm*
Churches and convents
→ *Most churches are only open during services:
7–10am and 6–10pm.*

EATING OUT

Tapas bars
Most Sevillians eat out on tapas (a type of appetizer) which they nibble standing at the bar. For something more substantial, ask for a *media ración* (half portion), *ración* (full portion) or *plato combinado* (meat or fish with vegetables or salad.

Restaurants/tapas bars
Some tapas bars have a back room offering set and

CITY PROFILE

- Capital of Andalusia;
Spain's 4th largest city
- 750,000 inhabitants
- Warm springs: 82°F;
hot summers:
95°F–104°F; mild falls
(77°F) and winters (59°F).

Mini glossary

Mudéjars: Muslims who
remained in Andalusia
after the Christian
Reconquest. The artistic
style they developed
(12th–16th c.) combined
Renaissance, Islamic and
Gothic influences.
Plateresque: Spanish
Renaissance style of
sculpted ornamentation
resembling ornate
silverware.

DISTRICTS OF SEVILLE

WWW.

Seville online
→ www.andalucia.com
Information on Andalusia.
→ www.sol.com
→ www.sevilla5.com
Two of the city's best sites.

Cyber centers
Workcenter (**D** A3)
→ C/San Fernando, 1
Tel. 954 21 20 74 Mon–Fri
7am–11pm; Sun 3–11pm
Alfalfa 10 (**B** C3)
→ Plaza Alfalfa, 10
Tel. 954 21 38 41
Daily 9am–1am
Cibercenter (**C** B2)
→ C/Julio César, 8
Tel. 954 22 88 99
Mon–Fri 9am–9pm

TOURIST OFFICES

→ Aeropuerto San Pablo
Tel. 954 44 91 28
Mon–Fri 9am–8.30pm; Sat
10am–6pm; Sun 10am–2pm
→ Santa Justa Station;
Av. Kansas City

Tel. 954 53 76 26
Mon–Fri 9am–8pm;
Sat–Sun 10am–2pm
→ Av. de la
Constitución, 21 (**A** C5)
Tel. 954 22 14 04 Mon–Fri
9am–7pm; Sat 9am–2pm,
3–7pm; Sun 9am–2pm
→ C/Arjona, 28 (**C** C3)
Tel. 902 19 48 97 Daily
9am–3pm (2pm Sat–Sun)

TELEPHONE

Telephone codes
UK/US to Seville
→ 00 (UK) or 011 (US) + 34
(Spain) + 9-digit number
Seville to UK/US
→ 00 44 (UK) or 00 1 (US)
+ number (without the '0'
for UK numbers)
Useful numbers
Medical emergencies
→ 061
Police
→ 091
Information
→ 1003 (national info) and
1025 (international info)

Lost property
→ Almasa, 21
Tel. 954 21 50 64
Tel. 954 42 04 03 (Tussam)

DIARY OF EVENTS

Public holidays
→ Jan 1, Jan 6 (Epiphany),
Feb 28 (Andalucia Day),
Maundy Thursday, Good
Friday, May 1, Aug 15, Oct 12
(national holiday), Nov 1,
Dec 6 (Constitution Day),
Dec 8 (Festival of the
Immaculate Conception),
Dec 25.
February
Carnival
→ Second or third week
Processions and concerts;
Baile de los Seises (13th
century): ten boys (there
used to be six) sing and
dance in the cathedral.
The dance is also
performed during the
festivals of Corpus Christi
and the Immaculate
Conception (Dec 8).

Marathon
→ Second Sun
March–April
**Festival de Música
Antigua**
Festival of traditional
music at the Teatro Lope
de Vega (**D** B3), the Teat
de la Maestranza (**C** E1),
and in some churches.
Semana Santa
→ Palm Sun to Easter Su
**Feria de Abril and start
the bullfighting season**
→ One-two weeks after
Easter
Late May–early June
Famous pilgrimage of th
Virgen del Rocío.
→ Thu before Whitsun
Feria del Corpus Christi
→ Sun after Whitsun
Corpus Christi
procession.
August
**Fiesta de la Virgen
de los Reyes**
→ Aug 15
Procession of the patro
saint of Seville.

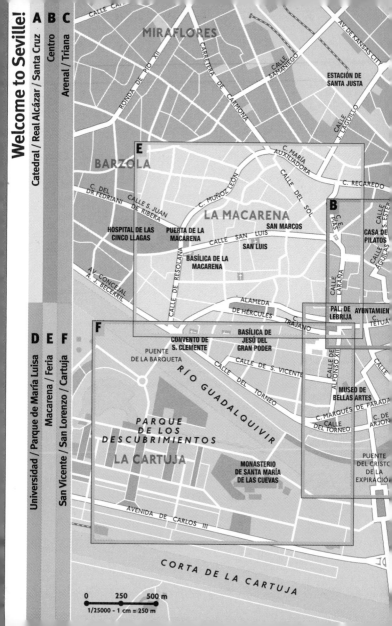

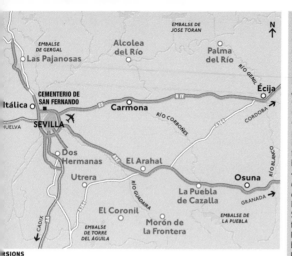

EXCURSIONS

Cementerio de San Fernando
→ *Northeast of Seville (bus no. 10 from Plaza de la Encarnación or B1 from Arco de la Macarena)*
On the outskirts of the city, this flower-filled cemetery planted with palms and cypresses is the pantheon of flamenco and *corrida*.

Itálica
→ *About 6 miles northeast of Seville (bus from Plaza de Armas)*
Founded in 206 BC by Scipio Africanus, the first Roman town on the Iberian Peninsula and birthplace of the emperor Hadrian. See the large amphitheater, vast baths and magnificent mosaic floors of the villas.

Carmona
→ *About 21 miles east of Seville (bus from Plaza de Armas)*
This 5,000 year-old city, surrounded by ramparts, stands above the valley of Los Alcores with its alcazars, churches, convents and squares that look like stage sets.

Osuna
→ *About 60 miles east of Seville (bus from Prado de San Sebastián)*
An ocher and white village surrounded by Roman walls. Thirteen religious sites including the imposing Hermitage de San Arcadio (17th c.).

Écija
→ *About 62 miles east of Seville (bus from Prado de San Sebastián)*
Roman town with magnificent baroque domes and bell towers.

...nday 8am–2pm
ps and coins.

adillo de Artesanía (**C** B1)
→ *del Duque de la Victoria, la Magdalena*
at 10am–10pm
es and handmade
ry from Asia and
America.

ado de Triana (**C** D3)
→ *del Altozano*
ue 8.30am–2.30pm,
n; Sat 8.30am–3pm
clothes, knick-knacks.
ado de la Feria (**E** C3)
Feria . Daily 8am–3pm
market.

WS AND EVENTS

old of the free
ly, *El Giraldillo*, from
st offices, some hotels
ourist sites. It gives
s of shows,
tions, concerts etc.
tral (**B** B6)
elázquez, 12
4 22 82 29

Mon-Sat 11am–2pm, 5–9pm
Booking office for *corridas*, football matches and shows (concerts, theater, dance).

Corrida
Bullfighting season
→ *Easter Sun–October*
La Maestranza bullring (**C** D2)
Daily bullfights during the Feria. After the Feria and throughout the summer are the *novilladas*: bullfights during which young *toreros* fight bulls under three years old.

Tickets
Available from the bullring, Plaza de Toros, and La Teatral booking office. €21–125 depending on where you sit (shade or sun).

Flamenco
Throughout the year great flamenco artists perform at venues throughout the city. See *El Giraldillo* for details.

Tablaos
Top quality flamenco shows where tourists and the initiated rub shoulders.

Shows generally start at around 9pm and 11pm.
El Patio Sevillano (**C** D2)
→ *Paseo de C.Colón, 11*
Tel. 954 21 41 20
The *tablao* of choice.

Peñas
You'll find the real soul of flamenco in these *aficionados*' (enthusiastic fan) clubs. For information, see:
Peña Piez Plomo (**F** E2)
→ *C/Darsena, 22*
Tel. 629 10 24 10
(Aurelia Abelar)

Football
Sevillians are mad about football, and with good reason – the city has two top-ranking teams, each with their own stadium.
Estadio Benito Villamarín (Real Bétis Balompié)
→ *Av. de la Palmera* (**D** E2)
Tel. 954 61 03 40
Estadio Ramón Sánchez Pizjuán (Sevilla Fútbol Club)
→ *Av. Eduardo Dato*
Tel. 954 53 53 53

…cessions across the
… during Holy Week
…oke the emotions of
… Passion of Christ.
… 58 brotherhoods
…ry the statues of their
…tron saints – real
…asures of religious art –
…ough the streets on
…sos (floats). You can
… to watch from the
…nds on the Plaza de
…n Francisco or follow
… nazarenos (penitents)
… foot. Official route:
… Campana, Calle
…erpes, Plaza de San
…ncisco, Avenida de
… Constitución, the
…hedral (guides on sale
…ross the city).

PUENTE ISABEL II

PASO (FLOAT) DURING THE SEMANA SANTA

FERIA DE ABRIL

This festival is an incredible two-week period of public celebration to mark the arrival of spring. On the fairground of the Real, in southwest Seville, the *casetas* (tents) echo to the sound of Andalusian songs and dancing throughout the night. At dawn, the *paseo de caballos* – a procession of horses and riders in Andalusian gypsy costume – passes through the narrow streets. The first bullfight of the season, at the Maestranza bullring, opens the festival.

…a carte menus.

…staurants
…t as numerous as the
…rs and often more
…pensive.

…ossary of
…linary terms
…ño: dressing
…a plancha: grilled
…horno: baked
…calao: cod
…cadillo: sandwich
…brales: a sort of blue
…neese
…brillas: small snails
…acina: cooked meats
…oquetas: cheese
…roquettes with ham and
…échamel sauce
…iso: dish served in sauce
…mo: spare ribs (pork)
…r ribsteak (beef)
…orcilla: black pudding
…eso: cheese
…lleno: stuffed, filled
…vuelto: scrambled eggs
…ith vegetables or other
…llings
…lpico: seafood salad
…lmorejo: thick gaspacho

Solomillo: meat fillet
Ternera: veal.

Smoking laws
Since 2006 smoking has been banned in all public places and this is adhered to in the majority of cases. Restaurants larger than 1,000 sq. feet are obliged to provide a smoking area but not all have done so as yet. Check the signs at establishment entrances.

SHOPPING

Department stores
Corte Inglés
Mon-Sat 10am–10pm
→ Plaza del Duque
de la Victoria, 10 (**F** F1)
Tel. 954 59 70 00
→ Plaza de la
Magdalena, 1 (**C** B1)
Tel. 954 59 70 10
→ C/Luis Montoro, 122
Tel. 954 57 14 40

Shopping malls
Plaza de Armas (**C** B3)
→ Tel. 954 90 82 82

Situated in the former neo-Mudéjar train station.
Nervión
→ C/Luis de Morales
Tel. 954 98 91 31
A temple (100,000 sq. feet) to ultramodern shopping.

Spanish brands and labels
Nearly always cheaper in Spain than elsewhere.
Zara (**F** F1)
→ Pl. del Duque de la
Victoria, 1 Tel. 954 22 10 15
Adolfo Dominguez (**B** B6)
→ C/Sierpes, 2
Tel. 954 22 65 38
Mango (**D** C4)
→ C/Asunción, 30
Tel. 954 279 667
Camper (**B** C6)
→ C/Tetuán, 24
Tel. 954 222 811

Convent confectionery
The nuns living in walled convents sell homemade confectionery through *torneos*, revolving wooden stands that protect them from prying – and profane

– eyes. Not to be missed!
Convento
de San Leandro (**B** B2)
→ Plaza San Ildefonzo, 1
Tel. 954 22 41 95
Yemas (pastries made with egg-yolk).
Convento
de Santa Paula (**E** D2)
→ C/Santa Paula, 11
Tel. 954 53 63 30
Marmalades.
Convento
de Santa Inés (**E** F3)
→ C/Doña María Coronel, 5
Tel. 954 22 31 45
Pastries.
El Torno (**A** B6)
→ Pl. del Cabildo
Tel. 954 21 91 90
Confectionery and hand-crafted items (lace, baby clothes etc.) made by nuns.

Markets
El Jueves (**E** C3)
→ C/Feria. Thu mornings
Antiques. The city's oldest market.
Mercadillo de la Plaza
del Cabildo (**A** B6)

PLAZA VIRGEN DE LOS REYES

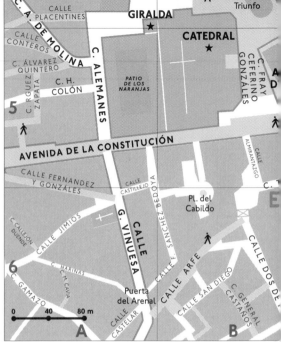

REAL ALCÁZAR

★ **Giralda** (A A4)
→ *Entrance C/Fray
Ceferino via the cathedral*
Tel. 954 21 49 71
*Winter: Mon-Sat 11am-6pm;
Sun 2.30-6pm;
Summer: Mon-Sat 9.30am-
4pm; Sun 2.30-6pm*
A symbolic tower – a
Renaissance bell tower
added to the 12th-century
Moorish tower of the Great
Mosque – embodying the
history of Seville. It serves
as a landmark for the huge
cathedral and offers an
unrivaled view of the city
and the interlaced design
of the flying buttresses from
the top (318 feet). It was
named after the weather

vane in the form of a figure
of Faith ('Giraldillo').
★ **Catedral** (A B5)
→ *Same opening times
as La Giralda*
The builders working on
the cathedral believed
that the people who saw it
would think they were mad.
The Gothic-Renaissance
church (1402–1509), built
on the site of the Great
Mosque, was the largest in
Christendom (425 feet
by 250 feet) until it was
superseded by St Peter's
in Rome. The richly ornate
interior has finely carved
vaulting, slender columns
and a host of treasures.
Also, a 17th-century rood-

screen in marble, jasper
and bronze, paintings by
Murillo, Zurbarán and
Valdés Leal, the tomb of
Christopher Columbus
(1900) and a remarkable
65-foot Flemish altarpiece
(1525) decorated with
thousands of polychrome
figures. You leave via the
Patio de Los Naranjos,
where the Muslims
performed their ritual
ablutions. Also worth
seeing is the Capilla Real,
a jewel of Renaissance
architecture (access Plaza
Virgen de los Reyes).
★ **Plaza Virgen
de los Reyes** (A A4)
Although usually filled with

horse-drawn carriage
square offers an unriv
view of La Giralda. Yo
also see the exquisite
century lantern-fount
and the lavish baroqu
entrance of the Palac
Arzobispal (1704).
★ **Real Alcázar** (A C
→ *Pl. de Triunfo*
Tel. 954 50 23 23
*Winter: Tue-Sat 9.30am
Sun 9.30am-5pm;
Summer: Tue-Sat 9.30a
5pm; Sun 9.30am-1.30*
This labyrinthine pala
begun by the Moors i
AD 844 and extended
Christian rulers from
blends Moorish, Gotl
Renaissance and bar

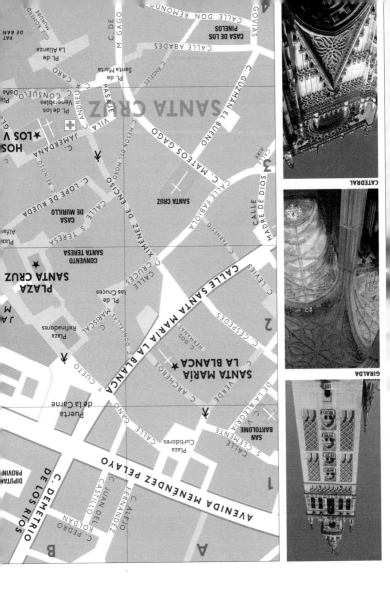

The historic heart of Seville harbors such architectural jewels as the huge Gothic cathedral, the distinctive minaret-bell tower (La Giralda), and the Real Alcázar, a delicately crafted Mudéjar palace set in jasmine-scented gardens. Further north are the narrow, winding streets of Santa Cruz, the old Jewish quarter. Charming little squares planted with orange trees, white façades with wrought-iron balconies and flower-filled patios are part of the Andalusian charm that still attracts tourists in their thousands. What could be more pleasant than to wander – and even lose yourself – in this picturesque district?

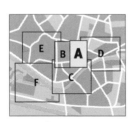

CASA ROBLES

348 CORRIENTES

RESTAURANTS

Bar Modesto (A B2)
→ *C/Cano y Cueto, 5*
Tel. 954 41 68 11
Daily 9am–2am
Enjoy lunch or dinner on the terrace opposite the Gardens of Murillo, near the church of Santa María la Blanca. A huge selection of Andalusian specialties including *fritura modesto* (fried fish). Set menu €17.50.

MOS (A D1)
→ *Av. Málaga, 6*
Tel. 954 532 910 Mon-Sat noon–4pm, 8pm–midnight
One of only a few Thai restaurants, housed in a hotel built by Aníbal González in 1929. Aromatic and fragrant dishes served amongst orchids and buddhas. À la carte €25.

La Albahaca (A B2)
→ *Plaza Santa Cruz, 12*
Tel. 954 22 07 14 Mon-Sat 1–4pm, 8pm–midnight
A very select restaurant with three (pink, blue and green) dining rooms in a 1930s townhouse. An inventive blend of Andalusian and Basque cuisine. Set menu €27.

Casa Robles (A A5)
→ *C/Álvarez Quintero, 58*
Tel. 954 21 31 50
Daily 1–4.30pm, 8pm–1am

(tapas served all day)
A classy, gastronomic restaurant serving Sevillia cuisine (and a favorite wit the Spanish royal family). Set menu €48. Only a stone's throw away: Roble Placentines (C/Placentine 2) for a more informal mea and Robles Tapas for... tapas (C/Conteros, 12).

TAPAS RESTAURANT

Peña Bética Puerta de la Carne (A A2)
→ *C/Santa María la Blanca,*
Tel. 954 53 76 89
Daily 11am–midnight
The favorite haunt of Real Bétis supporters, and the best place to watch footba at the weekend. It has a large, shady terrace opposite Santa María la Blanca. Bingo nights on Friday and Saturday. Set menu €7.

Las Lapas (A C5)
→ *C/San Gregorio, 6*
Tel. 954 21 04 29
Daily 1–4pm, 8–11pm
A minute from the Alcázar. House specialties in a canteen-style room off the bar, and a lovely one off th street. Set menu €15.

348 Corrientes (A C2)
→ *Paseo de Cat. de Ribera, 5*
Tel. 954 98 80 44
Daily 7am–1am
With its photographs of

.LOS

COCO SEVILLA

POPULART

Gardel Rivero and its Fauvist color scheme, this establishment captures the air of the famous tango bar at 348 Corrientes, in Buenos Aires. Succulent meats imported from Argentina, served grilled or in a sauce (*guisos*). Andalusian dishes too. À la carte €15.

Cervecería Giralda (A A4)
→ C/Mateos Gago, 1
Tel. 954 22 74 35
Daily 9am–midnight
Established in 1934, this is one of the most sought-after restaurants in Seville for its location (at the foot of La Giralda), its Moorish-bath decor and its tapas. Dining area for a sit-down meal. À la carte €20.

TAPAS BARS

Bodega Santa Cruz (A B4)
→ C/Rodrigo Caro, 1
Tel. 954 21 32 46
Daily 8am–midnight
You have to fight to place your order at the bar, and with good cause: great paella, *fideos a la marinera* (seafood pasta) and *sangre encebollada* (blood sausage with onions).

Las Teresas (A B3)
→ C/Santa Teresa, 2
Tel. 954 21 30 69 *Daily*
10am–4pm, 6pm–midnight
Las Teresas has been in the same family since 1870. The decor – bullfighting posters, rustic tables and *azulejos* – is as traditional as the cuisine. Specialties: *chacinas* (cold, cooked meats) from Huelva and fried fish.

BATHS

Baños Arabes (A A3)
→ C/Aire, 15
Tel. 955 01 00 24 *Daily 10am–2am (book ahead)*
Steam and the fruity scents of soothing oils emanate from the entrance of these baths. Massages and facial treatments… but first enjoy a tea on the roof terrace, with views over La Giralda.

FLAMENCO BARS

Los Gallos (A B2)
→ Plaza Santa Cruz
Tel. 954 21 69 81 *Daily 8–10pm, 10.30pm–12.30am*
This is mostly a tourist haunt, so it may not be the place to experience *el duende*, the special magic that unites dancers and *aficionados*. Even so, Los Gallos is one of the best *tablaos* (stages) in Seville and the shows (singing, dancing) are excellent.

El Tamboril (A B2)
→ Plaza Santa Cruz
Daily 5pm–3am
At midnight, the crowd gathers in silence to listen to the *Salve Rociera*, the breathtaking prayer to the Virgin Mary sung *a cappella*. Then it's time for the whirling rumbas and *sevillanas* to begin.

SHOPPING

Calenteria (A B2)
→ C/Cano y Cueto, 7
Tel. 954 41 22 56
Mon-Sat 8am–1pm, 4–8pm; Sun 7.30am–1pm
For three generations this family-run store has been proudly claiming it offered the best churros in town. And it may well be right.

Horno de San Buenaventura (A B5)
→ Av. de la Constitución, 16
Tel. 954 92 32 64 *Daily 7.30am (9am Sun)–11pm;*
Synonymous with tradition and exacting standards, this delicatessen, established in 1898, has five branches in Seville. Old-world gifts, impeccable service and delicacies to take away (cheese, wine, *chacinas*). Meals and snacks are also served throughout the day.

Coco Sevilla (A B3)
→ C/Ximénez de Enciso, 2
Tel. 954 21 45 32
Daily 11am–8.30pm
Andalusian craftsmanship updated and adapted to suit modern tastes by the joint talents of four French and Spanish craftsmen. Hand-painted silk shawls (*mantones*), fans with abstract designs, and jewelry and pottery at prices to suit every purse.

Felix Antique Poster (A B5)
→ Av. de la Constitución, 12
Tel. 954 21 80 26 *Mon-Fri 10.30am–12.30pm, 5–9pm; Sat-Sun 10.30am–12.30pm*
A dazzling selection of posters of bullfights and flamenco, and of 20th-century advertisements.

Populart (A B3)
→ Pasaje Vila, 4
Tel. 954 22 94 44 *Daily 10.30am–12.30pm, 5–9pm*
Traditional and modern ceramics from Triana and elsewhere.

Mercadillo de la Plaza del Cabildo (A B6)
→ Sun 8am–2pm
On Sunday, there's a stamp and coin market in this very pretty semicircular 'square'. The rest of the week you can hunt for bargains in the antique stores under the arcades.

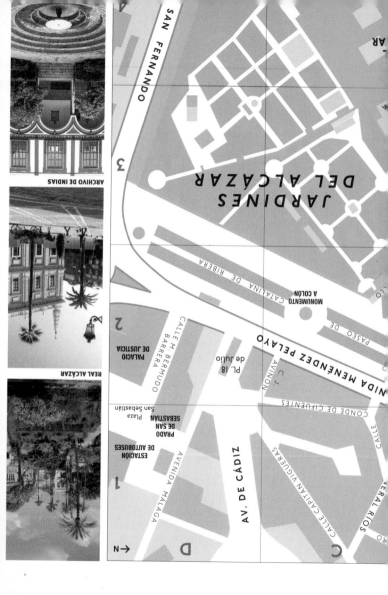

PLAZA SANTA CRUZ

SANTA MARÍA LA BLANCA

cture. In spite of this e of styles, the skill Mudéjar architects ed the Alcázar with rall unity and y. The spectacular th of rooms, with offered ceilings, (small courtyards), oil arches, gilded work and olored *azulejos*, are of the 'Arabian '. In the cool gardens eries of terraces, ins and pathways red with cypresses, and magnolias. See ite pavilion (*cenador*), y Charles V (1543) e 17th-century maze.

★ Archivo de Indias (A B5)

→ *Av. de la Constitución, 3*
Tel. 954 50 05 30
Mon-Fri 9am–3pm
Since 1785, the former Sevillian trade center (16th century) and Academy of Art (1660–74), founded by Murillo, has housed over 40,000 documents and archives dating from the the Spanish conquest of America. The portraits and writings of Cortés, Magellan and Pizarro which adorn the main hall bear witness to this illustrious era. The grand pink and grey marble staircase opens onto two floors with a vast patio area

flooded with light.

★ Hospital de los Venerables (A B3)

→ *Pl. de los Venerables, 8*
Tel. 954 56 26 96
Daily 10am–2pm, 4–8pm
A 17th-century hospice built for retired priests, and a masterpiece of Sevillian baroque architecture. Frescos by Juan and Lucas de Valdés Leal in the church and a 19th-century patio decorated with *azulejos*.

★ Plaza Santa Cruz (A B2)

With its white-and-orange façades, this is possibly the district's most typical square. In the center is the Cerrajería (1692), a

magnificent wrought-iron cross decorated with silhouettes of preachers, angels and demons.

★ Santa María la Blanca (A A2)

→ *C/Santa María la Blanca, 5*
Tel. 954 41 52 60 Mon-Fri
10am–10.30am, 4.30–7pm
The austere façade of this former synagogue disguises the baroque exuberance of the interior, which has influenced artists as far afield as South America. Cherubs, floral garlands and other stuccowork motifs provide a striking contrast with a very somber *Last Supper* (1650) by Murillo.

CALLE SIERPES

SAN JOSÉ

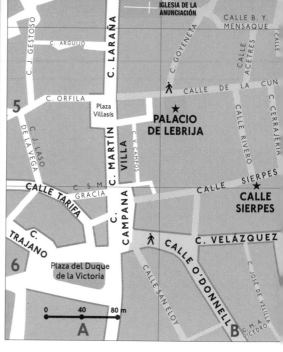

★ **Plaza Nueva** (B D6)
This vast, 19th-century style rectangular square is a popular meeting place for Sevillians. Sit on one of the benches and watch the world go by under the watchful eye of the statue at the center of the square of Ferdinand III, who reconquered Seville in 1246.

★ **Ayuntamiento** (B D5)
→ *Plaza Nueva*
Tel. 954 59 01 01
Guided tours: Tue-Thu 5.30pm and 6pm; Sat noon-1pm
The Plaza San Francisco offers the best view of the exquisite façade teeming with gods, ancient heroes

and strange creatures rendered in the pure Plateresque style (1527). Access to the magnificent state rooms of the town hall is via the 19th-century neo-Renaissance wing on the Plaza Nueva. Don't miss the coffered vault carved with 35 effigies of the kings of Spain (16th century) in the Sala Capitular Baja.

★ **Plaza San Francisco** (B D5)
The most public square in Seville, the scene of executions during the Inquisition and, since time immemorial, a station on the route of the Holy Week

processions (official stands are erected). Opposite the Ayuntamiento is the sober façade (1597) of the former tribunal building (Audiencia).

★ **Calle Sierpes** (B B5)
This popular, pedestrian shopping street is crowded – except during the hottest hours of the day. It is the sort of irresistibly old-fashioned street where you keep meeting the same people as you wander up and down. An ideal place to feel the pulse of the city, do some shopping and have tea at one of the many tempting patisseries.

★ **San José** (B C5)
→ *C/Jovellanos, 10*
Tel. 954 22 32 42
Mon-Fri 7.30am-12.30,
6-8.30pm
Beyond the terracotta sculptures of the ent the ornate interior is of 18th-century baro architecture. In the a lavish altarpiece is a with cherubs and sai watching over Joseph

★ **Palacio de Lebrija** (B B5)
→ *C/Cuna, 8*
Tel. 954 21 81 83
Mon-Fri 10.30am-1.30,
4.30-7.30pm (4.30-7.3
winter); Sat 10am-2pm
This 15th-century ma

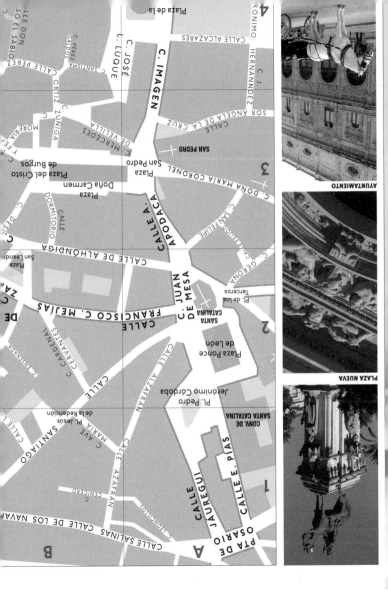

AYUNTAMIENTO

PLAZA NUEVA

Bordered by store windows and pedestrianized to make them even more attractive, the Calle Sierpes and surrounding streets appear to be dedicated to the god of trade. In the quieter, meandering streets to the east, half-open doorways offer glimpses of peaceful patios decorated with *azulejos*. Charming squares invite you to enjoy a drink on a café terrace or simply sit on one of the benches: Plaza San Francisco, illuminated by the Plateresque façade of the town hall, the Ayuntamiento; Plaza del Salvador, resplendent with the pink façade of its church; and Plaza de Pilatos, beautified by the exquisite palace it shares its name with.

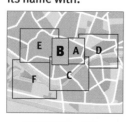

BARBIANA

ANTIGUA BODEGUITA

TAPAS RESTAURANTS

Barbiana (**B** C6)
→ C/Albareda, 11
Tel. 954 22 44 02
Daily 9am–noon, 1–4.30pm, 8pm–midnight
A little corner of Sanlucar de Barrameda in Seville. The waiters, like the wine and the food, all come from this village on the Guadalquivir estuary. Manzanilla (a type of sherry), fish, and seafood are given pride of place. The prawn tortilla is really good. À la carte €15.

Patio San Eloy (**B** A6)
→ C/San Eloy, 9
Tel. 954 22 11 48 Fri-Sat 11.30am–midnight; Sun-Thu 11.30am–5pm, 6.30–11.30pm
Tapas and *montaditos* (small sandwiches) to take away or to enjoy on the *azulejos*-covered steps at the back of the room.
À la carte €15–17.

Antigua Bodeguita (**B** C5)
→ Plaza del Salvador, 6
Tel. 954 56 18 33 Daily noon–4pm, 8pm–midnight
The decor is straight out of the legendary Spanish baroque *comedias*...
Outside, on the Plaza del Salvador, sip a *caña* (draft beer) or *tinto de verano* (red wine and lemonade)

standing at the huge barrels. Always busy. À la carte €18.

Victoria Eugenia (**B** A5)
→ Plaza Villasis (corner of Cuna). Tel. 954 22 74 59
Daily 12.30–4.30pm, 8pm–midnight
Housed in a building by Aníbal González. Enjoy *bacalao* (cod) in all its forms: raw, marinated, grilled, with garlic preserv with tomatoes, etc.
À la carte €18.

Bar Estrella (**B** D4)
→ C/Estrella 3
Tel. 954 22 75 35
Mon-Sat 9–12.30am (kitchen 12.30–4.30pm)
Has attracted a following from all over the city since 1936. *Cabrales* (local blue cheese) croquettes and *berenjenas tapadas* (home-grown eggplant).
À la carte €20.

San Marco (**B** B5)
→ C/de la Cuna, 6
Tel. 954 21 24 40 Daily 12.30 4.30pm, 8pm–12.30am
Near the Palacio Lebrija is another 18th-century palace owned by Ansano Ramaciotti, a Florentine who loves Seville. Cuisine with a delicious Tuscan flavor. Around 3pm and 10pm it is invaded by the Seville smart set, so it is best to book in advance.
Set menu €30.

LA CAMPANA

EL BESTIARIO

VICTORIO & LUCHINO

TEAROOM

La Campana (B A6)
→ C/Sierpes, 1/3
Tel. 954 22 35 70
Daily 8am–10pm
Seville's most famous patisserie dates from 1885, as do the old fortune-telling scales. Waitresses in black with lace aprons, and waiters in striped waistcoats will help you choose from the vast range of *polvorones rellenos* (filled cookies), *yemas* (pastries made with egg-yolk), candied fruits and chocolates.

FLAMENCO BARS, CLUBS

Around the Plaza del Salvador (B C5)
Seething with crowds around 1–3am on a Saturday night, this plaza is where young people gather to party, with their own supplies of beer and wine – it is quite a sight.
La Carbonería (B D2)
→ C/Levies, 18
Tel. 954 21 44 60 Daily 8pm–3.30am (shows 11pm)
Opened the day after Franco's death, this vast club promotes culture and enjoyment in a spirit of democracy. Guitar and flamenco lessons during

the day, and two to three shows in the evening (consecutive or simultaneous): flamenco (*puro* or *nuevo*), blues, jazz, rock and world music. An exciting venue where customers and artists alike mingle and chat at the huge tables.
El Bestiario (B D6)
→ C/Zaragoza, 33
Tel. 954 21 34 75
Mon–Thu 3pm–3am;
Sat–Sun 3pm–6am
Very chic yet relaxed *bar de copas*, where it seems that everyone is part of the same big group of friends. Colored spotlights illuminate the dancers as they lose themselves in pop, electro and rock.
Trinity (B D6)
→ C/Madrid, 5
Tel. 954 22 49 70
Daily 10am–1am
The cozy pub of a hotel, where the pieces of furniture come from Dublin to recreate the decor of Trinity College, the oldest university in Ireland. Large choice of beers and cocktails.

SHOPPING

Calzado Mayo (B C4)
→ Plaza Alfalfa, 2
Tel. 954 22 55 55
Mon–Fri 10am–2pm,

5–8.30pm; Sat 10am–2pm
A leading manufacturer of flamenco shoes. The great dancer Cristina Hoyos shops here.
Blasfor (B B6)
→ C/Sierpes, 33
Tel. 954 22 76 61
Mon–Fri 9.45am–1.30pm, 4.40–8.30pm;
Sat 9.45am–1.30pm
In 1933, Juan Foronda opened the first workshop in Seville to make shawls (*mantones*), mantillas and fans (until then made in the villages) and sold them in this store. Today, there are five of these workshops in the city. Handmade lace and hand-embroidered silk.
Victorio & Luchino (B D6)
→ Plaza Nueva, 10
Tel. 954 50 26 60
Mon–Sat 10am–8pm
Since the 1970s, Victorio and Luchino have been creating fashion that blends contemporary style with Andalusian tradition, all shown off to its best advantage by the sublime lighting.
→ C/Sierpes, 87
Dresses for young girls.
Cuquicastellanos (B C6)
→ C/Rosario, 8
Tel. 954 56 09 96 Mon–Fri 10am–2pm, 5–8.30pm; Sat 10.30am–2pm, 5–8.30pm

A fine selection of shoes, clothes and accessories by Spanish designers, as well as some more affordably-priced fashion.
Marietta Artesanía (B A2)
→ C/Santiago, 8
Tel. 954 22 77 42
Mon–Fri 5–8pm
An attractive mix of new and reasonably priced 'antiques'. Worth a visit just to see Marietta's studio in a beautiful town house with a central patio.
Compás Sur (B C4)
→ C/Cuesta del Rosario, 7a
Tel. 954 21 56 62
Mon–Sat 10.30am–2.30pm, 5.30–10pm (8.30pm Sat)
The store in Seville for Spanish music: flamenco, *marchas* of the Semana Santa, bullfighting paso dobles, or *coplas* (folksongs). Also sells records, books, music scores and castanets. Has a record booth and offers guitar lessons too.
Vinoteca (C C2)
→ C/Águilas, 6
Tel. 954 21 65 49 Daily 11am–4.30pm, 7–11.30pm
Wines from across Spain and choice dishes that fuse the traditional with the contemporary: sea urchin caviar, salmon with ewe's cheese... to take out or eat in.

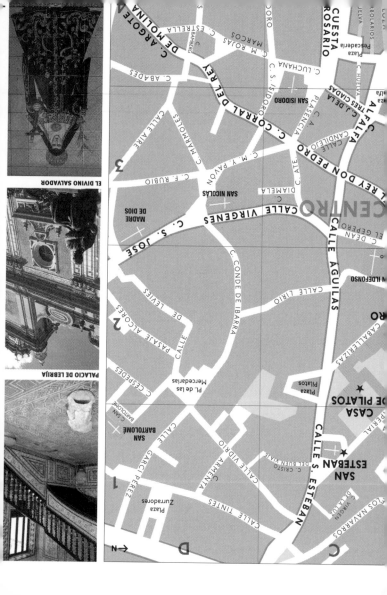

EL DIVINO SALVADOR

PALACIO DE LEBRIJA

CENTRO

CUESTA DEL ROSARIO

C. ARGOTE DE MOLINA

Plaza Pescadería

C. M. ROJAS
C. BAMBERG
C. ESTRELLA
C. MARCOS
C. S. ISIDORO
C. LUCHANA

C. ABADES

C. CORRAL DEL REY

CALLE ABARE
C. MÁRMOLES
SAN ISIDORO

PLASENCIA
CALLE CANDILEJO
C. DE LA
ALFALFA

C. ATE
C. M. Y PAVÓN

C. REY DON PEDRO

C. F. RUBIO
DIAMELA

SAN NICOLÁS
C. DEÁN
EL GÉPERO

CALLE VÍRGENES

C. S. JOSÉ
MADRE DE DIOS

CALLE ÁGUILAS

C. CONDE DE IBARRA

CALLE LIRIO

DE LEVÍES

PASAJE ALCORES

CALLE
CABALLERIZAS

Plaza Pilatos

CASA DE PILATOS

CALLE S. ESTEBAN

SAN ESTEBAN

C. CÉSPEDES

Pl. de las Mercedarias

SAN BARTOLOMÉ

CALLE

CALLE VIDRIO

C. CRISTO DEL BUEN VIAJE

GARCI PÉREZ

C. ARMENTA

Plaza Zurradores

CALLE TINTES

N →

3

2

1

D

C

CASA DE PILATOS

SAN ESTEBAN

ted in eclectic style provides a brief ary of the history of usian art. The main se, with its three is typically Sevillian. oot is a Roman c floor from Itálica oove, a Mudéjar d ceiling. The walls corated with 17th- y Triana *azulejos*.

ivino dor (**B** C5)
→ *a del Salvador*
21 16 79
for restoration works
er grandiose and mental baroque (1674–1712) built site of a mosque

in an attempt to outdo the Muslim architects. Inside, two magnificent altarpieces by the master of rococo, Cayetano de Acosta (1711–80), and, on a silver altar, a moving *Jesús de la Pasión* (1619) by the Sevillian sculptor Juan Martínez Montañés.

★ **Iglesia del Convento de San Leandro** (**B** B2)
→ *Plaza San Idelfonso, 1*
Tel. 954 22 41 95
Daily 7–8.30pm; all day on the 22nd of each month
The single-nave church has two amazing altarpieces by Juan Martínez Montañés, dedicated to San Juan Bautista and San Juan

Evangelista (1621–32). Also, a statue of Santa Rita de Casia, patron saint of lost causes, draped in gold-embroidered black velvet. Worth visiting on the 22nd of the month, when worshippers bring her flowers. Pastries (*yemas*) made by the nuns are sold through the *torneo* (revolving wooden stand).

★ **Casa de Pilatos** (**B** C2)
→ *Plaza Pilatos, 1*
Tel. 954 22 52 98
Daily 9am–6pm
This jewel of a palace, completed in 1521, marked the first station on one of the city's *vías dolorosas*. But there is nothing

austere about its ancient sculptures, loggias, columns, galleries and fountains inspired by Renaissance, Gothic and Mudéjar styles. Wander in the idyllic garden (at its best in spring) with its wonderfully haphazard flowers and exotic plants.

★ **San Esteban** (**B** C1)
→ *C/San Esteban*
Tel. 954 42 20 54
Mon 8–9am, 10am–1pm;
Tue-Sat 8–9am, 8–9pm;
Sun 10.30am–noon
See the altar decorated with *azulejos* and the painted altarpiece signed by Zurbarán beneath the Mudéjar-Gothic vault.

RÍO GUADALQUIVIR

NUESTRA SEÑORA DE LA O

★ **Torre del Oro** (**C** E1)
→ *Paseo de Cristóbal Colón*
Tel. 954 22 24 19
Tue-Fri 10am–2pm; Sat-Sun and public hols 11am–2pm
The defensive Almohad 'Golden Tower' (13th century) was once linked to a 'Silver Tower' in Triana, on the far bank, by chains that prevented the movement of river traffic. Named after the gold *azulejos* that once adorned its walls, today it houses a small maritime museum.

★ **Hospital de la Caridad** (**C** E1)
→ *C/Temprado, 3*
Tel. 954 22 32 32
Mon-Sat 9am–1.30pm,

3.30–7.30pm; Sun and public hols 9am–1pm
This former hospice for the poor has a dazzling white façade despite its decor of blue-and-white Dutch tiles. Its completion was due to the generosity of Miguel de Mañara (1627–79), a reformed libertine who provided the inspiration for Don Juan. In the chapel, masterpieces include two 'vanities' (1672) by Juan de Valdés Leal and a magnificent *Entombment* (1673) by Pedro Roldán.

★ **Plaza de Toros de la Maestranza** (**C** D2)
→ *Paseo de Cristóbal Colón, 12*

Tel. 954 22 45 77
Daily 9am–7pm
The acoustics in this spectacular ocher, red and white bullring allow you to hear the snorting of the bull and the swish of the *muleta* (matador's stick). Mérimée and Bizet knew what they were doing when they chose the 'cathedral of bullfighting' as the setting for Carmen's tragedy. Today, her statue stands facing the theater. Beneath the terraces are the Museo Taurino (with its dazzling costumes and bullfighting images) and the chapel where the *toreros* pray before the *corrida*.

★ **Paseo de Cristób Colón** (**C** D2)
One of the city's most pleasant avenues run along the banks of th Guadalquivir between San Telmo and Isabel bridges. Take in the vi of the Torre del Oro, L Maestranza and Trian

★ **La Magdalena** (**C**
→ *C/San Pablo*
Tel. 954 22 96 03
Mon, Tue, Thu 10.45am noon; Sun 8–11am (ma
La Magdalena is one Seville's finest baroqu churches. Before you glance up at the dazz *azulejos*-covered dom Inside, see Leonardo

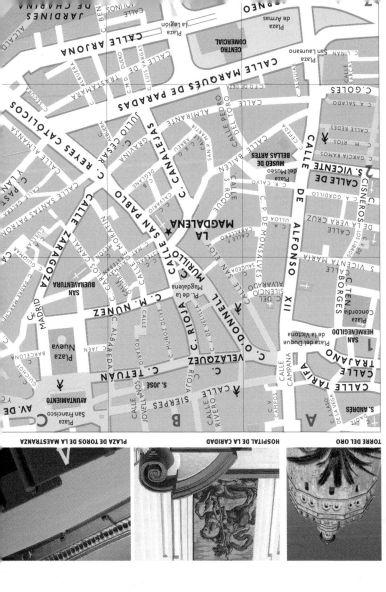

TORRE DEL ORO

HOSPITAL DE LA CARIDAD

PLAZA DE TOROS DE LA MAESTRANZA

Two very different districts on opposite sides of the river. On the right bank, El Arenal, the former port district, is famous for its magnificent Maestranza bullring, the Hospital de la Caridad, and the Torre del Oro. On the left bank, Triana – for a long time linked to Seville by a floating bridge – is proud of its heritage and identity as a working-class district (*barrio*) populated by gypsies, sailors and potters. The Calle Betis, with its many café terraces, is the hub of this busy district. Even so, the sound of flamenco echoes through the quieter streets that lie beyond.

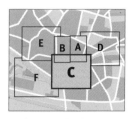

AS-SAWÏRAH

SOL Y SOMBRA

RESTAURANTS

As-Sawïrah (C C2)
→ *C/Galera, 5*
Tel. 954 56 22 68
Tue-Sat 2–4pm, 9pm–midnight; Sun 2–4pm
A Moroccan restaurant run by Spaniards born in Morocco. Couscous, tajines (slow-cooked meat and vegetable stews) and Spanish wines served in a spacious dining room decorated in hues of blues and reds. Set menu €13.

La Mandragora (C C3)
→ *C/Albuera, 11*
Tel. 954 22 01 84 Thu-Fri 2–4pm; Sat 9.30–11.30pm
There's nothing special about the decor but the food is certainly good. Very inventive vegetarian cuisine. À la carte €20.

TAPAS RESTAURANTS

Sol y Sombra (C C4)
→ *C/Castilla, 149*
Tel. 954 33 39 35 Daily 1–4pm, 8.30pm–midnight
A real Ali Baba's cave of Sevillian gastronomy, with a decor of bullfighting posters, and hams hanging from the ceiling. On the menu, the chef's own creations and his mother's best recipes: *solomillo al ajillo* (sirloin

steak with garlic), *ortiguillas* (sea anemones) *tagarninas* (wild edible thistles). À la carte €13.

Las Golondrinas (C D3)
→ *C/Antillano Campos, 26*
Tel. 954 33 16 26 Daily 1–4.30pm, 8pm–12.30am
The Arcas family has been welcoming customers here since 1951. The à la carte menu is small but each dish is a gem: highlights include the grilled cuttlefish, the carrots *à l'orientale* and mushrooms in garlic cream. Carte €13.

Faro de Triana (C D3)
→ *Puente de Isabel II*
Tel. 954 41 48 64
Daily 8am–midnight
Housed in a former 19th-century lighthouse that once guided fishermen on the river. Unrivaled view of the Maestranza and the Torre del Oro. Andalusian cuisine. Set menu (Mon–Thu) €10.

Bodeguita A Romero (C D1)
→ *C/Antonia Diaz, 19*
Tel. 954 22 39 39
Tue-Sun noon–1am
Right next to the bullring, this is a favorite venue for *aficionados* as, on the day before a fight, the *toreros* themselves call in for a drink after the *sorteo* (draw for the bulls). Delicious *punta de*

TRIANA AZULEJOS

PACO ALVAREZ

olomillo (sirloin steak)
nd *cola de toro* (oxtail).
 la carte €15–20.

**Taberna del
Alabardero (C** C1)
→ C/Zaragoza, 20
Tel. 954 50 27 21
Daily 1–4.30pm,
8.30pm–midnight
Magnificent 19th-century
palace now owned by
the school of catering.
The ultimate Spanish inn
that is all things to all
people: a deli, tearoom,
tapas bar, gastronomic
restaurant, luxury hotel.
A la carte €35.

TAPAS BARS

Casa Ruperto (C F4)
→ Av. de Santa Cecilia, 2
Tel. 954 08 66 94
Sat-Thu 8am–midnight
Although slightly outside
the center, this place is
worth a detour as Ruperto
has become known as the
'partridge king'. The
cabrillas (small snails) are
equally famous. The food
is consistently excellent.

Los Angeles (D D2)
→ C/Adriano, 2
Tel. 954 22 81 46
Daily 8.30am–10.30pm
This bar/tearoom regales
its customers with its
homemade *churros*, tapas
and pastries at all hours.
Great savory breakfasts.

FLAMENCO BARS,
CLUBS, THEATER

**Teatro de la
Maestranza (C** E1)
→ Paseo de C. Colón, 22
Tel. 954 22 65 73
Andalusia's main theater
and opera house was built
for the Expo '92.

Boss (C F2)
→ C/Fortaleza, 13
Tel. 954 27 42 86
Wed-Sat 10pm–7.30am
Elaborate lighting,
designer bars and a huge
screen in the city's largest
disco. All kinds of music.
Smart dress compulsory.

Casa Anselma (C D4)
→ C/Pagés del Corro, 49
Tel. 954 50 13 42
Mon-Sat from 11.30pm
Anselma, the mistress
of the house, certainly
knows how to call a tune
and dance a *sevillana*.
Here, couples don't dance
unless they know the
principles of the art.
Reserve in advance.

Lo Nuestro (C E2)
→ C/Betis, 31/A and 31/B
Tel. 658 80 90 03
Daily 10pm–5am
Two flamenco bars with
a distinctive style,
masterfully managed by
José Carlos: at 31/B for
flamenco *puro*, which is
best enjoyed seated; at
31/A for *sevillanas*.

SHOPPING

Ceramics/azulejos

The specialty of Triana.
Stores galore in the
potters' district on the
Calle Antillano Campos
and Calle Alfarería.

**Veinte Emilio
Garcia Ortiz (C** D3)
→ C/Antillano Campos, 10
Tel. 954 33 35 99 Mon-Fri
9am–2pm, 5–8pm;
Sat 9am–1pm; ring the bell
if you find the door closed
Tile-makers for three
generations. Handmade.

Paco Alvarez (C D3)
→ C/Castilla, 22
Tel. 954 34 32 22 Mon-Sat
10am–1.30pm, 5–8pm
Flamenco and festival
dresses, mostly by Paco
Alvarez, combining
traditional and modern
design in a wide range of
colors and light, easy-to-
wear fabrics.

Rocío Trastallino (C D3)
→ C/Castilla, 22
Tel. 954 34 12 30 Mon-Sat
10am–2pm, 5.30–9pm
A former designer of
flamenco dresses, Rocío
Trastallino has turned
her hand to Andalusian-
inspired off-the-peg
fashion. Stylish evening
wear.

Akiaba (C D3)
→ C/Castilla, 10
Tel. 954 33 14 70 Mon-Sat

10am–1.30pm, 5–8.30pm
Myriam Gallego can now
count Princess Maxima
of Holland among her
many fans, since the latter
fell for the Andalusian
designer's bags while
visiting Seville. The shop
also sells leather holdalls
by the Argentinian designer
Peter Kent.

Sombreros (C D1)
→ Av. de la Constitución, 2
Tel. 954 22 24 55 Mon-Sat
10am–2pm, 5–8pm
Distinguished suppliers of
bullfighters' costumes
since 1935. Mere mortals
will have to settle for the
made-to-measure hats.

**Huerta
de San Vivente (D** D2)
→ C/Adriano, 18
Tel. 954 56 38 82 Mon-Sat
10am–2pm, 5–8.30pm
Beautifully made, colonial
style Andalusian
beechwood furniture.
Vast choice of smaller
objects too, including an
unusual wall lamp in the
shape of a salamander.

El Caballo (C D1)
→ C/Antonio Díaz, 7
Tel. 954 21 81 27 Mon-Sat
10am–1.30pm, 5–8.30pm
Andalusian leather store
selling saddles alongside
luxurious and stylish suede
items.

**Also, Centro comercial
Plaza de Armas (C** B3)

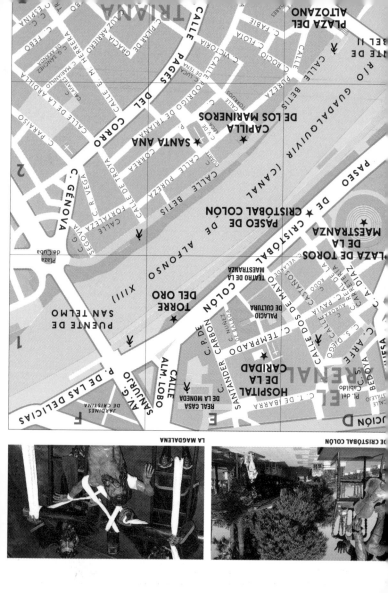

DE CRISTÓBAL COLÓN

LA MAGDALENA

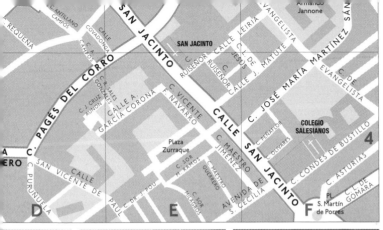

EL ALTOZANO

CAPILLA DE LOS MARINEROS

SANTA ANA

a's octagonal dome
ted by a drum, the
wood altarpiece,
by Lucas Valdés,
ntings by Zurbarán
rillo. The Capilla de
ta Angustia has a
Descent from the
Roldán studio)
g physical and
al states of trance.

lquivir (C C4)
*ral boat companies
from the foot of
e del Oro*
eared for its raging
the river has also
source of prosperity
ut it Seville may not
ecome the 'gateway

to America'. Today, it is less
unpredictable and offers
the prospect of peaceful
boat trips and beautiful
views of the city.

**★ Nuestra Señora
de la O (C** C3)
→ *C/Castilla, 30*
Tel. 954 33 75 39
Daily 10am–1pm, 6–9pm
The real *Nuestra Señora
de la O*, sculpted by La
Roldana, daughter of
Pedro, disappeared around
1930. This replica, with
its glass tears and sad
expression, is just as
popular. In the chapel is
the authentic *Nazareno*
(1670) by Pedro Roldán
and decorative *azulejos*.

**★ Plaza
del Altozano (C** D3)
At the Triana end of the
Puente Isabel II, *azulejos*
highlight the dome of the
Capilla del Carmen (1928)
by Aníbal Gonzáles. Below,
the proud bronze figures
of a gypsy woman and the
matador Juan Belmonte.
The square reflects the true
spirit of Triana, the home
of ceramics, flamenco and
great *toreros*.

**★ Capilla
de los Marineros (C** E2)
→ *C/Pureza, 53*
Tel. 954 33 26 45
*Mon-Sat 9.30am–1pm,
5.30–9pm; Sun 9.30am–1pm*
This is the shrine of the

anonymous *Virgen de la
Esperanza de Triana* which,
along with 'La Macarena',
is one of the city's most
venerated Madonnas. The
baroque statue has a
distinctly gypsy-like look.

★ Santa Ana (C E2)
→ *C/Vasquez de Leca, 12*
Tel. 954 27 08 85
*Mon Fri 11.30am–1pm,
7–8.30pm (9pm summer);
Sat-Sun 7–8.30pm*
This Mudéjar-Gothic church
was Seville's first cathedral
(1276). In the choir is
a wonderul painted
Renaissance altarpiece
with ceramic effigies of
Santa Ana and Santa
Isabel.

PARQUE DE MARÍA LUISA

PLAZA DE AMÉRICA

★ Palacio de San Telmo (D A4)

→ Av. de Roma
Tel. 955 03 55 00

The school of navigation was built in 1682 to instruct the future conquerors of the New World. It later became the residence of the dukes of Montpensier, and is now the seat of the regional government of Andalusia (Junta). The 'altarpiece' entrance (1733) consists of a lavish composition in which the allegorical figures of Science – dominated by San Telmo, the patron saint of seafarers – stand on a balcony supported by strong Atlantes.

★ Hotel Alfonso XIII (D A3)

→ C/San Fernando, 2
Tel. 954 91 70 00

The most famous palace in Seville was built in neo-Mudéjar style for the 1929 Exhibition. The central patio, which echoes to the tinkling of a fountain, is surrounded by broad corridors offering views of the perfectly balanced brick and ceramic decor from every angle. Take a drink here or simply walk around the lobby.

★ Casino de la Exposición (D B3)

→ Av. María Luisa
Tel. 954 23 26 39

Temporary exhibitions
The Pabellón de Sevilla, also built for the 1929 Exhibition, houses a casino and theater. Its beautiful neo-baroque architecture has an outdated charm.

★ Universidad / Fabrica de Tabacos (D A3)

→ C/San Fernando
Tel. 954 55 10 00
Mon-Fri 8am–9pm;
Sat 8am–1pm

The former tobacco factory (1725) covers an area of around 7 ½ acres. Above the entrance is an effigy of an American Indian smoking tobacco. In the 19th century, the factory and its thousands of *cigarreras*

captured the romant imagination and pro the inspiration for Mérimée's – and Biz heroine Carmen. Tod university students h replaced the *cigarrer*

Plaza de España (D
A semicircular neo-Renaissance palace flanked by two Italian towers. The towers o onto an arcaded gall that overlooks a serie ceramic designs ded to the Spanish provin a little canal complet boats and a central fountain. This master by the architect Aníbal González is by far the

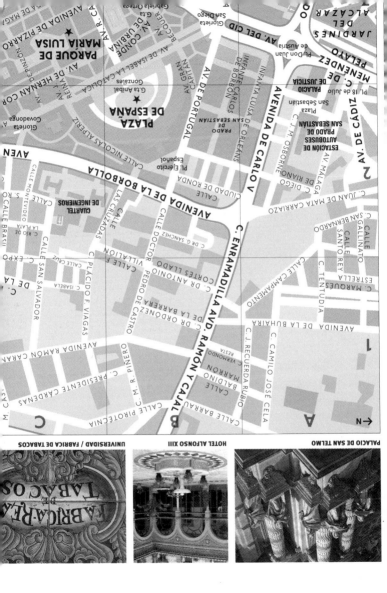

AVENIDA DE MAGA
AVENIDA DE PIZARRO
AV. DE DENZON
AV. DE HERNÁN COR
AV. DE HERNÁN COR

★ PARQUE DE MARÍA LUISA

Glorieta A Covadonga

AV. R. CA
AV. DE URBINA
BECQUER
AV. DE ISABEL LA CATÓLICA
CAPITÁN GONZÁLEZ

Gabriela Ortega

Glorieta San Diego

JARDINES DEL ALCÁZAR

DE MENDEZ PELAYO

AV. DEL CID

Pl. Don Juan de Austria

G.ta Aníbal González

★ PLAZA DE ESPAÑA

Pl. 18 de Julio

JUSTICIA
DE
PALACIO DE JUSTICIA

DE CÁDIZ

2

AV. DE CÁDIZ

INFANTA LUISA DE BORBÓN
INFANTE CARLOS DE BORBÓN
AV. DE PORTUGAL

PRADO DE SAN SEBASTIÁN
AV. DE CARLO V
AVENIDA DE CARLO V

Plaza San Sebastián
C.J. M. SAN SEBASTIÁN
PRADO DE SAN SEBASTIÁN
ESTACIÓN DE AUTOBUSES

AV. MÁLAGA
C. DIEGO DE RIAÑO
C. J. M. OSBORNE

AVEN

CALLE NICOLÁS ALPÉRIZ
PL Ejército Español

CALLE MONTEVIDEO
CALLE BRASIL
CALLE S.

AVENIDA DE LA BORBOLLA

CIUDAD DE RONDA

C. JUAN DE MATA CARRIAZO

CUARTEL DE INGENIEROS

LAS CRUZADAS
CALLE DOCTOR

CALLE CRUZ
C DR G SÁNCHEZ

CALLE CAMPAMENTO

CALLE GALLINATO
CALLE SAN BERNARDO
SANTO REY

C. ISABELA

PLÁCIDO F. VIAGAS
CALLE SAN SALVADOR
C. DE LA
C. EXPO
C. RO DE LA PAJA

CALLE LLADÓ
PEDRO DE CASTRO
C. ANTONIO
C. DR ORDÓÑEZ
VILLALÓN
CORTES LLADÓ

MARQUES
C. TENTUDIA
ESTRELLA

AVD. RAMÓN Y CAJAL
C. ENRAMADILLA

AVENIDA RAMÓN CARAN

C. PRESIDENTE CÁRDENAS

C. M. R. PINEDO
VERONDO
C.J. RECUERDA RUBIO

CALLE BALDINO MARRÓN
CAMILO JOSÉ CELA

1

CALLE BARRAU
C. M.

CALLE PROTECNIA
CALLE PIROTECNIA

A

N →

C

B

PALACIO DE SAN TELMO

HOTEL ALFONSO XIII

UNIVERSIDAD / FÁBRICA DE TABACOS

FÁBRICA-REA
DE
TABACOS

In 1929, the Hispanic-American Exhibition was held only a stone's throw from the tobacco factory and the Palacio de San Telmo. The project was supervised by architect Aníbal González who also created the Plaza de España and Plaza de América in his favorite historicist style. Between the two *plazas* lies the romantic Parque de María Luisa and, to the east, a series of mansions (El Porvenir), also built in the late 1920s. Across the river you will see the façades of the modern buildings of Los Remedios, a district built on a grid layout in the 1970s. The Calle de Asunción there is the epitome of elegant shopping.

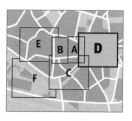

EL ACEITE

LA RAZA

RESTAURANTS

Manolo León (**D** D2)
→ C/Juan Pablos, 8
Tel. 954 23 71 09 Daily
1.30–5pm, 9pm–midnight
Andalusian cuisine
served in a spacious
dining room decorated
like a countryside inn:
red floor tiles, old beams
supporting a low ceiling
and 19th-century
paintings. *Chacinas*
(cold, cooked meats)
from Huelva and delicious
guisos (cooked dishes in
a sauce). À la carte €20.

El Aceite (**D** D2)
→ Corner of C/Valparaíso
and C/Juan Pablos
Tel. 954 62 92 14
Daily 1pm–midnight
Mediterranean cuisine
with a strong Andalusian
flavor whose open secret
is written in large letters
on the restaurant sign;
everything is prepared
using the very best olive
oil (available to buy)
made by a small regional
producer. À la carte €25.

Egaña Oriza (**D** A3)
→ C/San Fernando, 41
Tel. 954 22 72 54 Daily
1.30–3.30pm, 9–11.30pm
An elegant restaurant
boasting impeccable
service and reputedly the
best in Seville. A blend of
Basque and Andalusian

nouvelle cuisine served in
a huge 1920s-style
veranda. À la carte €40.

TAPAS RESTAURANTS

Victor (**D** D2)
→ C/Felipe II
Tel. 954 61 89 35
Daily 12.30–4.30pm,
8.30pm–12.30am
Victor, the young
Andalusian chef, adds
his personal touch to the
Sevillian cuisine – try
the delicious *almogrote*
(soft cream cheese with
tomato and garlic). Tapas
are eaten sitting at one of
the huge barrels; more
elaborate dishes are
served in the small dining
room. Friendly service.
À la carte €12.

**La Colonial de Vinos
y Viandas** (**D** D2)
→ C/Valparaíso, 13
Tel. 954 61 47 10 Tue–Sun
1–4pm, 8.30pm–midnight
A real wine bar with
delicious Spanish wines
beyond the classic Riojas
and Riberas del Duero.
The menu varies
according to demand
and the inspiration of
the gourmet owner-chefs.
Selection of Cuban cigars.
À la carte €15.

Julia-Los Monos (**D** D3)
→ C/Glorieta de México

ORIZA

TEATRO LOPE DE LA VEGA

LA NORIA

*Tel. 954 61 50 27
Bar: daily 7am–1am;
Restaurant: daily 1–4.30pm,
9pm–midnight*
For tapas, find a place at
the long crowded bar.
Meals, served in the
elegant restaurant with
its red drapes, are more
expensive. Good, but not
especially inventive,
cuisine. Set menu €10;
à la carte €20.

La Raza (D B3)

→ *Av. de Isabel la Católica, 2
Tel. 954 23 20 24 Daily
1–4pm, 8pm–midnight*
Next to one of the
pavilions built for the
1929 Exhibition. Inviting
terrace with wrought-iron
chairs and mosaic tables
in the shade of well-
established trees. Tasty
tapas. Meals served in
two stylish dining rooms.
À la carte €21.

TAPAS BARS

Cinco Jotas (D C4)

→ *C/Asunción, 10
Tel. 954 28 23 40
Mon-Fri 8am–10.30pm;
Sat 10am–3.30pm*
A chain of tapas bars set
up in 1983 to distribute
chacinas from Jabugo –
cold, cooked meats
produced by the 100-year-
old Sanchez Romero
curing factory. Cinco Jotas

is a guarantee of quality.
Its ham is produced from
free-range pigs fed on
acorns and aromatic
plants, which give it its
slightly nutty flavor.

THEATER, ATTRACTIONS

Teatro Lope de Vega (D B3)

→ *Avenida de María Luisa
Tel. 954 59 08 53*
Italian-style theater in the
Pabellón de Sevilla built
for the 1929 Exhibition.
Drama, music and dance.

La Noria (D B2)

→ *Jardines del Prado de San
Sebastián. Tel. 954 61 88 46
Daily 10am–9pm*
Suspended over Plaza
de España, this ferris
wheel, at close to
200 feet high, offers
a vertiginous view over
the city.

BARS, CLUBS

Bilindo (D D2)

→ *Plaza de América
Tel. 954 62 61 51 Oct-Jan:
8.30am–8pm; Feb-May:
8.30am–midnight; June-
Sep: 8.30am–dawn*
On the enchanting Plaza
de América, this kiosk
with tables serves snacks
at all hours. On summer
evenings it becomes an

open-air disco playing
Latin-American music.

Aduana (D D3)

→ *Av. de la Raza
Tel. 954 61 42 99
Daily midnight–8am (closed
June-Sep) www.aduana.net*
A favorite with young
Sevillians who dance the
night away to all kinds
of music.

VouleZBar (D B1)

→ *Edificio Viapol C/Baldino
Marrón Tel. 607 67 11 75
Mon-Wed 4pm–3am;
Sat-Sun 4pm–7am*
Mix the mellowness of
Bali with the mood of
Ibiza for one of the best
copas bars in Seville. Two
beautiful rooms edged
with white sofas and with
marble bars look onto a
dance floor set in a private
garden. Chic and
glamorous. Salsa on Wed;
flamenco on Fri nights.

O'Neil (D B1)

→ *Edificio Viapol
C/Baldino Marrón
Tel. 954 64 31 04
Tue-Sun 1.30–4.30pm,
8.30pm–midnight;
Sun 1.30–4.30pm*
A screen showing the
Betis matches occupies
the central spot in this
vast pub. Around the main
area, steps lead off to
small booths where you
can snack on chips and a
beer. Reasonably priced.

SHOPPING

Agua de Sevilla (D A3)

→ *C/San Fernando, 3
Tel. 954 50 15 38
Daily 10am–1pm, 5–9pm*
Jasmine, lemon, orange
blossom... the summer
scents of Seville and the
magic formula for an eau-
de-toilette that launched a
perfume range and luxury
items: leather goods, art
deco, jewelry and fashion.

Sedicci (D C4)

→ *C/Asunción, 16
Tel. 954 28 45 47
Mon-Fri 10am–2pm, 5–9pm;
Sat 11am–2pm*
A wide range of designs
reflecting the femininity
and stylishness of Sevillian
women. Brilliantly put
together by former lawyer
María Luisa Hernandez.

El Sombrero de Tres Picos (D A4)

→ *Plaza de Cuba, 8
Tel. 954 28 34 58 Mon-Fri
10am–1.30pm, 5–8pm;
Sat 10.30am–1.30pm*
From classic *sombreros* to
the most unusual of hats.
Definitely worth a visit!

Don Algodón (D C4)

→ *C/Asunción,
Tel. 954 27 13 85 Mon-Sat
10am–1.30pm, 5–8.30pm*
Dazzling fabrics and
flattering cuts for classic,
Andalusian-style fashions
with a fanciful twist.

AVENIDA DE LA RAZA

CALLE DE TARFIA

AVENIDA PAEZ DE RIVERA

CALLE LORENZO DE SEPULVEDA

DE SANTA TERESA

CALLE SOR GREGORIA

C. ISAAC PERAL

AVENIDA DE LA PALMERA

AVENIDA MANUEL SIUROT

AV. CARDINAL BUENO MONRE

CALLE CARDINAL BUENO MONRE

AVENIDA DE LA RAZA

AV. DE MOLINI

DELICIAS

ARTES
MBRES
ARES

Glorieta
de México

★ **PLAZA DE AMÉRICA**

**MUSEO
ARQUEOLOGICO**

AV. DE
ERITAÑA

RBOLLA

CALLE DEL PROGRESO

CALLE DE VALPARAISO

CALLE COLOMBIA

CALLE JUAN PABLOS

CALLE DE FELIPE II

EL PORVENIR

CALLE BOGOTA

CALLE CONDE GALVEZ

CALLE BADALOTOSA

CALLE ATECA

C. CARDENAL ILUNDAIN

CALLE DE LARA NIETO

C. PARODI

C. B. G. DO

GALLARDO

GALLARDO

C. JUAN DELARA NIETO

C. GENARO PARLARDE

C. TABLADILLA

CALLE ANTONIO MAURA MONTANER

CALLE
CARD. ILUNDAIN

CALLE
GENARO PARLARDE

C. E. J. M. LARA

C. PEDRO SALINAS

C. JORGE GUILLEN

AVENIDA
RAMON CARANDE

AVENIDA TETINOS

CALLE JUAN DE LA COSA

F

E

D

2

1

PUENTE DE LAS DELICIAS *(CANAL DE ALFONSO XIII)*

DALQUIVIR

AV. SAN LUCAR DE BARRAMEDA

C. CURRO ROMERO

4

CALLE A. BIENVENIDA

D   E   F

0   75   150 m

DE ARTES Y COSTUMBRES POPULARES

MUSEO ARQUEOLÓGICO

COSTURERO DE LA REINA

…agant square created 1929 Exhibition. A …e walk for Sevillians.
…que de …Luisa (**D** C3)
…mantic park, with its …nt stream of horse-carriages, was …gned for the 1929 …tion. It includes the …ns of the Palacio de …lmo, given to the city …ía Luisa Fernanda …urbon in 1893. Shady …ays, islands …*tas*) planted with …nt species, pools, …ins and vast lawns …t an ideal place for …l. Don't miss the …ta, a sculpted group

of three female figures: Love Fulfilled, Love Deceived and Love Lost, which are dedicated to the Sevillian poet Bécquer.

★ **Plaza de América** (**D** D2)
Around this elliptical *plaza*, another masterpiece by Aníbal González, three buildings reflect the architectural styles of Seville: Mudéjar (Museo de Artes y Costumbres Populares), Plateresque (Museo Arqueológico) and Gothic (Pabellón Real). In the center is a pool bordered by tall palm trees and, at the far end, fountains that attract

flocks of white doves.

★ **Museo de Artes y Costumbres Populares** (**D** D3)
→ *Plaza de América, 3*
Tel. 954 23 25 76 Tue 2.30–8.30pm; Wed-Sat 9am–8.30pm; Sun 9am–2.30pm
A museum of Andalusian folklore, with reconstructed workshops (guitars, castanets, pottery), a beautiful collection of *azulejos*, and English china from the factory of La Cartuja (1841–1982).

★ **Museo Arqueológico** (**D** D2)
→ *Plaza de América*
Tel. 954 23 24 01
Tue 2.30–8.30pm;

Wed-Sat 9am–8.30pm; Sun 9am–2.30pm
Mosaics and Roman statuary from Itálica. In the basement, the Carambolo Treasure: a fabulous collection of solid gold, Phoenician-style jewelry (8th–7th century BC).

★ **Costurero de la Reina** (**D** B3)
→ *Paseo de las Delicias, 9*
Tel. 954 23 44 65
Mon-Fri 8am–7pm
This summerhouse (1890) in neo-Mudéjar-Andalusian style stood in the gardens of the Palacio de San Telmo and housed its dressmaking workshops. Wonderful at sunset.

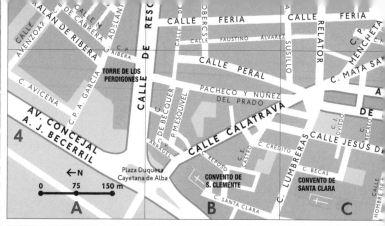

SAN MARCOS

SAN LUIS

BASÍLICA DE LA MACARE

★ Alameda de Hércules (E D4)

At the end of this broad, tree-lined avenue and square, statues of Hercules and Julius Caesar look down on passers-by from the top of their Roman columns. Work to provide walkways on the square is currently underway.

★ Calle Feria (E C3)

There is nothing flashy about this street which has a true feel of working-class Seville. Its small shops have a charming, old-fashioned simplicity, and the many furniture stores spill painted wood-and-cane chairs onto the

sidewalk. On Thursday mornings, the space is occupied by second-hand dealers hawking their wares at the city's oldest market.

★ San Pedro (E F3)

→ C/Doña María Coronel, 1
Tel. 954 22 91 24
Daily 7–8.30pm

This church, with its brick Gothic-Mudéjar façade was built after the reconquest of Seville in the 14th century. It contains a splendid 16th-century ceramic retable depicting Purgatory and holy images (also 16th century) of Christ with the Virgin crying crystal tears at his feet.

★ Santa Catalina (E F2)

→ Plaza de los Terceros
Tel. 954 21 74 41
Closed for renovation

A 14th-century church built, as so often in Seville, on the site of a mosque. Inside are two masterpieces: the Capilla Sacramental (18th century), a baroque chapel by Leonardo de Figueroa; and a *Christ* (1684) by Pedro Roldán (Capilla de la Exaltación). More unusual is the commemorative painting to Santa Lucía, the patron saint of the partially sighted, hung with hundreds of real and fake eye glasses.

★ Convento de Santa Paula (E D

→ C/Santa Paula, 11
Tel. 954 53 63 30
Tue-Sun 10am–1pm

One of the city's few walled convents ope to the public – use th bronze knocker to announce your arriva the church isn't oper the small museum w rich collection was be when the monastery founded in 1483. In g cabinets, some spec baroque images of th Infant Jesus are displ next to death masks. There's a wonderful c on a par with Neapol

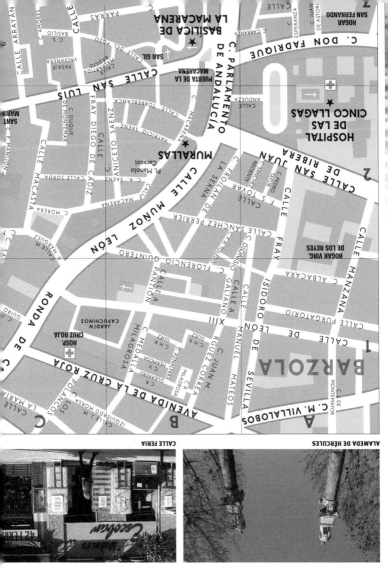

CALLE FERIA

ALAMEDA DE HÉRCULES

The district of La Macarena is the home of the city's most venerated Madonna. It is also regarded as the working-class heart of the 'real' Seville. Its narrow streets are set with architectural jewels: Mudéjar-Gothic churches, baroques sanctuaries – with San Luis as the crowning glory – and walled convents where you have to knock to buy confectionery. The busy Calle Feria, with its small stores and charming market, is a world apart from the nearby Alameda de Hércules, whose trendy stores and alternative clubs cater for the city's more bohemian elements.

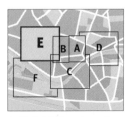

DIABLITO

RAYAS

RESTAURANTS

La Ilustre Victima (E D4)
→ C/Doctor Letamendi, 35
Tel. 954 38 94 90
Daily 9–2am
International cuisine – from traditional tapas, couscous, shawarma (beef or lamb marinated in yoghurt and spices) and enchiladas (stuffed tortillas), to vegetarian dishes. The atmosphere is reminiscent of a Pedro Almodóvar film set.
À la carte €11.

El Vegetarium (E E3)
→ C/Sor Ángela de la Cruz, 37. Tel. 954 21 61 03
Mon–Sat 2–4.30pm, and also 8.30–11pm Fri-Sat
The haunt of English-speaking travelers in need of a good, home-cooked vegetarian meal. Set lunch menu €9; à la carte €12.

Diablito (E D4)
→ Alameda de Hércules, 7
Tel. 954 37 74 61
Daily 1pm–1am
Everything here is designed to arouse the senses: vibrantly colored walls, lounge music and a menu leaning toward Tex-Mex. Open throughout the day for nachos, pizzas, salads and pasta if you find yourself suddenly famished. Always a

charming welcome.
À la carte €15.

TAPAS RESTAURANTS

El Rinconcillo (E E3)
→ C/Gerona, 40
Tel. 954 22 31 83
Daily 1pm–1.30am
You can tell by the worn floor tiles that the Rinconcillo has been around for a while. Established and run by the same family since 1670, it's a historic monument and one of the last bars-abacerías (bar-grocer's) in Seville. Andalusian cuisine: 'fresher than fresh' fish and salmorejo (thick gaspacho) to die for.
À la carte €15.

Bar Plata (E B3)
→ C/Resolana, 2
Tel. 954 37 10 30
Mon–Thu 5.30–1.30am; Fri-Sun open 24hrs
Coffered ceiling, wooden bar and well-trained waiters in a traditional bar opposite La Macarena. Try the eggplant pâté, and the lamb cutlets with Armagnac or roquefort cheese. À la carte €15.

El Bacalao (E F2)
→ Plaza Ponce de León, 15
Tel. 954 21 66 70
Tue-Sat noon–4.30pm,

MA ESTRELLA

MERCADO DE LA CALLE FERIA   **DADDO HOBBY**

8pm–midnight (12.30am Fri-Sat); Sun noon–4.30pm
The parent restaurant of a small Sevillian chain devoted to *bacalao* (cod). So good that it's often overcrowded. À la carte €20.

TAPAS BARS

Cerveceria Gonzalo Molina (E C3)
→ C/de Relator, 59
Daily noon–4pm,
8pm–12.30am
A very attractive bar over 100 years old. Also a popular venue for poetry readings and for listening to singer-songwriters (*cantautores*).

Yerba (E B1)
→ C/Medalla Milagrosa, 3
Tel. 954 35 10 07 Tue-Sun noon–4pm, 8pm–12.30am
Crowds gather here at all times of the day to enjoy the excellent tapas in this authentically Sevillian bar.

CAFÉS, ICE CREAM PARLORS

La Buena Estrella (E E4)
→ C/Trajano, 51
Tel. 620 94 56 17
Daily 9–3am
The affable atmosphere of the 'Lucky Star' stands out in a district that isn't always known for its

friendliness. A bar-cum-tearoom serving savory treats, delicious pastries and all kinds of black, green and flavored teas (rose, apple, melon) and coffees (vanilla, caramel).

Rayas (E F3)
→ C/Almirante Apodaca, 1
Tel. 954 22 17 46
Mon-Fri 3pm–midnight;
Sat-Sun noon–midnight
A sophisticated and stylish confectioner's selling quality chocolate and ice cream: 40 sorts of filled chocolates, truffles and pralines and every flavor of homemade ice cream imaginable.

BARS, CLUBS

Urbano Comix (E E2)
→ C/Matahacas Osorio, 5
Tel. 954 21 03 87
Daily 9.30pm–5.30am
In a quiet street, this all-night bar with a cartoon-style decor echoes to the strains of jazz, blues, soul, rock and Latin-American music.

Naima Café Jazz (E D4)
→ C/Trajano, 47
Tel. 954 38 24 85
Mon-Fri 3pm–3am;
Sat-Sun 4pm–3am
One of the few jazz clubs in Seville. The walls are decorated with black-and-white photos of the two

most famous Spanish jazz festivals: Vitoria and San Sebastian. The audience are only too delighted to indulge their passion over a drink.

Fun Club (E D4)
→ Alameda de Hércules, 86
Tel. 650 48 98 58
Thu-Sat midnight–6am; Fri-Sat concerts from 9.30pm
The giant graffiti decor here aptly reflects the district this club is located in. Listen to live, hip pop, rock and electronic music until dawn.

SHOPPING

Glam (E E4)
→ C/Amor de Dios, 27
Tel. 954 90 47 66
Mon-Sat 10am–1pm,
5–8pm
'Glam' for glamor: past and future fashions with a marked preference for the 1970s, and plastic and synthetic materials. Clothes and shoes.

Duplex (E C3)
→ C/Peris Mencheta, 22 B
Tel. 686 28 44
Mon-Fri 11am–2pm, 6–9pm;
Sat 11am–2pm
This quirky boutique selling clothes, brand-name sneakers, DJ equipment and records, is unique in Seville. You can even get your haircut in

the store's salon. The staff will answer all your questions about the latest releases in electro music.

Daddo Hobby (E D3)
→ C/Feria, 37
Tel. 954 38 15 76 Mon-Sat 10am–2pm, 5–9pm
Welcome to the world of Sevillian religious tradition... in miniature. Nativity figurines – Christs, Madonnas, penitents and Holy-Week floats (*pasos*) – available in kit form or assembled. A curiosity not to be missed.

Record Sevilla (E E4)
→ C/Amor de Dios, 27
Tel. 954 38 77 02
Daily 10.30am–2pm,
5–7pm
A record store of repute stocking flamenco, rock, hip-hop, tango... If you can't find what you're after, they will make a point of finding it for you. Also sells second-hand clothes concert tickets.

Mercado de la Calle Feria (E C3)
→ C/Feria, backing onto the Omnium Sanctorum
Mon-Sat 8am–3pm
A lovely market which reflects the working-class spirit of the area. Tuesdays ring out with the cries of the fish sellers... something well worth seeing and hearing.

SAN PEDRO

Plaza del Cristo
de Burgos

★ SAN PEDRO

M. DE VELILLA
SOR ÁNGELA DE LA CRUZ
C. ESPÍRITU SANTO

PALACIO
DE LAS DUEÑAS

CALLE CASTELLAR
CHORRUCO
C MIGUEL
CINCOENTAS
CAVALLINAS
C INFANTES
CHINCOENTES
C MARRAVILLAS

C. M DE
C. ALHÓNDIGA
CALLE DE
SANTA CATALINA
★ SANTA CATALINA
F. C. MEJÍAS

C. APODACA
CALLE DOÑA MARÍA CORONEL
C. FELIPE
GERONA

Plaza de
Los Terceros

C. BUSTOS TAVERA

AN LUIS

SAN MARCOS
★ SAN MARCOS

SANTA ISABEL
Plaza
Santa Isabel

HINIESTA
C. SOCORRO
C. DE CASTRO
C. PENUELAS

Plaza Ponce
de León

CONVENTO DE
SANTA CATALINA
Pl. Padre
Jerónimo
Córdoba

CALLE DEL SOL

A MACARENA
LA MACARENA
CALLE
S. PAULA
ASALE MALLOL

CALLE
2
AVE AZAFRÁN MARÍA
CALLE
JÁUREGUI
CALLE E. PÍAS

CALLE
SANTIAGO
CALLE
CERVANTES
CAMP
DE LOS LICÓRDIOS

C. DE LOS NAVARROS
PUÑON-
ROSTRO-

AVE
C. TENORIO
C. CONDE NEGRO

MATAHACAS OSARIO
C. CARLOS
C. BUITRÓN

CALLE DEL PINTO

C. VERONICA

CONVENTO DE
SANTA PAULA
★
CALLE DE LA ENLADRILLADA

P. del
Pelícano

CALLE DEL
PINTO

CALLE DE LOS
RÍOS
C. DE RECAREDO

CALLE ARROYO
VIRGEN DE GRACIA
Y ESPERANZA
C DEL REY

CALLE C.
LAGUILLO
CALLE
ARROYO

JARDINES
DEL VALLE
CALLE DEL VALLE

CALLE MARÍA
AUXILIADORA

C. MARTIRES
C VIUDA
DE LA TRINIDAD
C MARÍA ISABEL

CALLE
AMADOR DE LOS RÍOS
BILBAO
E. ESPERANZA
LOPE DE VEGA
CALLE
DE JÚPITER

C. ARROYO

C. J. LAGUILLO

CALLE
SALESIANOS
C. DR.
RELIMPIO
CALLE J. M
TORRES
C. DR.
J. TORRES

ESCUELAS
SALESIANAS

D

E

1

2

CONVENTO DE SANTA PAULA

SANTA CATALINA

DRO

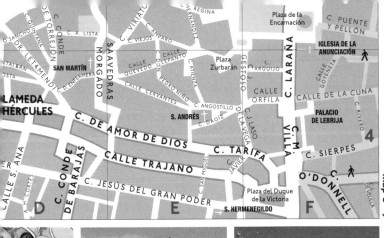

map 6

MURALLAS

HOSPITAL DE LAS CINCO LLAGAS

i – with a colorful of figurines. Before *ve*, stock up on *ledas* made by the of Santa Paula.

Luis (E D2)

an Luis
55 02 07
9am–2pm;
10am–2pm, 5–8pm
y Leonardo de
a for the Jesuits in
m of a Greek cross,
the most Roman of
's baroque churches
–1731). It has an
ng sculpted façade
dome covered in
os. The interior is
taking: a high dome
d by Lucas Valdés,

rich altarpieces, frescos depicting angels and the emblem of the Jesuits.

★ **San Marcos (E** D2)
→ *Plaza de San Marcos, 10 Tel. 954 50 26 16 Daily 7.30–8.30pm (mass 8pm)*
A 14th-century Mudéjar church with a Giralda-style bell tower. Its three bare, white naves make a change from the usual baroque extravagance. Two splendid sculptures: *San Marco* (17th century) and a recumbent figure of Christ (18th century).

★ **Basílica de la Macarena (E** B3)
→ *C/Bécquer, 1 Tel. 954 90 18 00*

Daily 9.30am–2pm, 5–9pm
The church was built in 1949 to house the *Virgen de la Esperanza*, the best known of Seville's Madonnas, sculpted by an unknown artist in the 17th century. The tears on her sorrowful face are diamonds. In the adjoining museum, see the finery that adorns the statue during Holy Week (jewelry, the embroidered cloak), the impressive *paso* (float) and the dazzling costumes donated by *toreros*.

★ **Murallas (E** B2)
The remains of the 12th-century Almohad fortifications stretch for

500 yards, from San Hermenegildo to the Puerta de la Macarena. Through this gateway, the symbol of the district, the kings of Spain used to enter the city.

★ **Hospital de las Cinco Llagas (E** A2)
→ *C/Parlamento de Andalucía. Tel. 954 59 21 00 Visits by appointment Mon-Tue 5–8pm*
Today, this former hospital (1545–1613), one of the most majestic Renaissance buildings in Seville, is the seat of the Andalusian parliament. The four patios and the church are fine examples of the Mannerist style.

CONVENTO DE SAN CLEMENTE

PUENTE DE LA BARQUETA

ISLA MÁGICA

★ Museo de Bellas Artes (F F2)
→ Pl. del Museo, 9
Tel. 954 22 07 90
Tue 2.30–8pm;
Wed-Sat 9am–8.30pm;
Sun 9am–2.30pm
Museum housed in a former convent brilliantly renovated (1612) by Juan de Oviedo. It holds one of the country's most important collections of Spanish and European art, from the Middle Ages to the 20th century, with major works of Sevillian baroque art by Pacheco, Murillo, Zurbarán and Valdés Leal. The impressive baroque staircase and 18th-century church decorated by Domingo Martínez provide a fitting backdrop for the works. On the second floor the 19th- and early 20th-century paintings illustrate Sevillian *Costumbrismo* (genre painting) and Romanticism. An ideal introduction to the history of Andalusian art.

★ San Vicente (F F2)
→ C/Miguel Cid, 1
Tel. 954 90 44 72
Mon-Sat 9.45–1045am,
7–9pm; Sun noon–1.30pm
Among the treasures in this 14th-century Mudéjar church are the altarpiece (1706) and an 18th-century *Christ* attributed to Pedro Roldán.

★ San Hermenegildo (F F1)
→ Pl. de la Concordia
Tel. 954 91 51 46
This disused church is all that remains of the Jesuit college founded in 1579. Stop to admire its beautiful oval lines and the dome decorated with stuccowork bas-reliefs attributed to Juan de Mesa. In 1823, it was the scene of a liberal uprising during which Ferdinand VII was deposed and war declared on France. Exhibitions held.

★ Basílica de Jesús del Gran Poder (F E1)
→ Plaza San Lorenzo, 13
Tel. 954 91 56 72

Daily 8am–2pm, 6–9p
(10pm Fri)
A specially built circu
chapel (1965) house
Seville's most venera
statue, the *Jesús del
Poder*, by Juan de Me
(1620). Is it really inv
with the 'great powe
makes the basilica o
the city's major spirit
centers? Absorbing t
silence in the chapel
walking along the co
behind the altar from
you can kiss the stat
heel, you begin to wo

★ San Lorenzo (F E
→ Plaza San Lorenzo
Tel. 954 38 69 56 Mon
Sat 8am–1.30pm (1pm

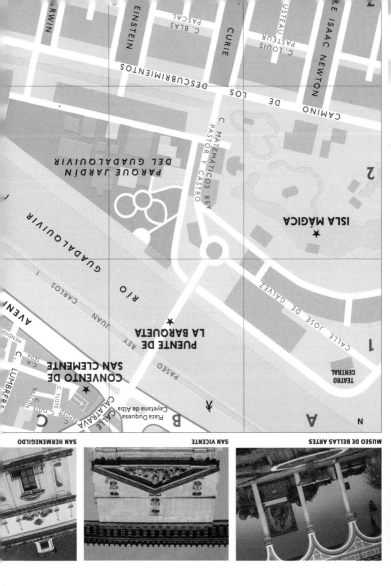

SAN HERMENEGILDO

SAN VICENTE

MUSEO DE BELLAS ARTES

The island-district of La Cartuja, in northwest Seville, was the site of Expo '92. Today, the futuristic exhibition pavilions have been turned into office blocks and the district seems fairly deserted, but it's well worth a visit. The 500-year-old monastery houses a center for contemporary art, and, in summer, there are café terraces on the banks of the Guadalquivir. On the far side of the river, traditional Seville reasserts itself. Beyond the Plaza del Duque de la Victoria, the preserve of the big department stores, lie the peaceful districts of San Vicente and San Lorenzo, with their Mudéjar and baroque churches and convents.

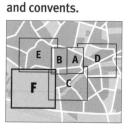

EGO

ANTIGUA ABACERÍA

RESTAURANT

Casa Manolo León (F D1)
→ Guadalquivir, 12
Tel. 954 37 37 35
Daily 1.30–5pm,
8.30pm–12.30am
The same Manolo León as at the Calle Juan Pablos (D D2). Eat on the pretty patio or in the rooms of an old townhouse. The à la carte menu gives pride of place to chacinas, and fish and meat prepared in traditional Sevillian style. An agreeable experience. À la carte €30.

TAPAS RESTAURANTS

Ego (F C1)
→ C/Calatrava
Tel. 616 68 42 06
Daily noon–12.30am
(kitchen noon–4pm,
9–11.30pm)
The artists of Alameda make a detour here to have their work displayed, and show future trends. The Hispano-Asian food and the orange-colored, retro-modern decor celebrate the crossover of these two cultures. Set menu €9.

El Sardinero (F E1)
→ Plaza San Lorenzo, 15
Tel. 954 38 94 24 Mon, Tue,
Thu–Sun 7am–midnight
A shady and spacious terrace on the Plaza San Lorenzo where you can watch the comings and goings of the pilgrims who come to pray to the 'Jesús del Gran Poder'.
For breakfast, very good tostadas aceite-jamón (toast with olive oil and cured ham). Paella on Sunday. À la carte €9.

Antigua Abacería de San Lorenzo (F D1)
→ C/Marqués de la Mina, 2
Tel. 954 38 00 67
Mon-Sat 9.30am–11pm
(8pm Tue-Wed)
A tiny bar-abacería-panadería (bar-grocer's-baker's) where you can stock up on good conserves and sample Ramón's original cuisine: lightly spiced peppers with melted cheese, chicken breast, carrots and beetroot in sweet-and-sour sauce. You'll need to book – there are only six tables.
À la carte €15.

Casa Ricardo (F D1)
→ C/Hernán Cortés, 2
Tel. 954 38 97 51
Mon-Sat 1–5pm,
8pm–midnight; Sun 1–5pm
The walls are covered from floor to ceiling with religious images and photos of famous

CAFE LATTE

MANUEL HERNANDEZ LEÓN

customers. There are no menus – the waiters recite the specialties of the day, which are always Andalusian. À la carte €17.

La Ribera de Cartaya (F E1)
→ C/Martínez Montañés, 5
Tel. 954 90 78 12 Daily 1.30–4pm, 8.30–11.30pm
Sublime seasonal cuisine. The focus is on *chacinas*, fish and wines from Huelva (the owners are from nearby Cartaya). Try the *pulpo feirado* (octopus on a bed of potatoes). À la carte €17.

Eslava (F D1)
→ C/Eslava, 3/5
Tel. 954 90 65 68
Tue–Sat noon–midnight; Sun noon–4pm
Booking is essential for the restaurant, and you also have to elbow your way to the bar to order a tapa. Andalusian cuisine with a French flavor – the wife of Sixto, the owner, is French. In summer, they only use vegetables and fruit from their own kitchen garden. À la carte €20.

TAPAS BARS

Amarillo Albero (F E1)
→ Plaza de la Gavidia, 5
Tel. 954 21 90 85

Daily noon–5pm, 8pm–midnight
Enjoy house specialties at the huge barrels that serve as tables: scallops, partridge eggs with ham or chorizo, and pork kebabs.

THEATER, CONCERTS, CLUBS

Auditorio de la Cartuja (F C3)
→ Camino de los Descubrimientos, Isla de la Cartuja
Tel. 954 46 07 48
This ultramodern complex was built for Expo '92. It hosts all the major singer-songwriter concerts along with Spanish and international band events.

Teatro Central (F A1)
→ Isla de la Cartuja
Tel. 955 72 00 03
Another major theater built in 1992, resolutely open to different periods, genres and cultures: jazz, flamenco, music, drama and modern dance.

La Imperdible (F D1)
→ Pl. San Antonio de Padua, 9
Tel. 954 90 54 58
Thu–Sun from 8pm
This is *the* alternative arts venue in Seville. Concerts of a high standard are performed by amateurs

in the Café Almacén. Videos, dance, music, drama and comedy performances in the two studios. Children's theater plays on Sat at 6pm.

Anima (F E1)
→ C/Miguel Cid, 80
Tel. 954 38 67 08
Daily 9pm–3am.
Closed Jan, Aug
Superbly decorated with ceramic tiles, this bar was opened by an Austrian who fell in love with Seville. It welcomes friends and artists after the curtain comes down at the shows in the area, which can make for a lively and sometimes heated atmosphere.

Antique Theatro (F B2)
→ C/Mat. Rey Pastor y Castro
Tel. 954 46 22 07
Thu–Sat midnight–dawn (daily in winter)
Two floors, a stage for concerts and an attractive modern decor: this is where serious Sevillian clubbers like to spend the night.

Cafe Latte (F E1)
C/ Jesús del Gran Poder, 83
Tel. 954 90 46 07
Daily 4pm–4am
A colorful and friendly bar with a reputation for great, homemade tarts. Rock and electro music.

SHOPPING

Librería Céfiro (F F1)
→ C/Virgen de los Buenos Libros, 1 Tel. 954 21 58 83
Mon–Fri 10am–1.30pm, 5–8.30pm; Sat 10am–1.30pm
An excellent bookstore in the 'street of the Virgin of good books'. With each purchase, Luis Salas, a specialist in Sevillian history, gives a bookmark inscribed with a poem.

Sevilla Musical (F E1)
→ C/Cardenal Spínola, 3 (plaza de la Gavidia)
Tel. 954 91 57 55 Mon–Fri 10am–1.30pm, 5–8.30pm; Sat 10am–1.30pm
Musical instruments, guitars and flamenco scores.

Manuel Hernandez León (F E1)
→ C/Teodosio, 95 A
Tel. 954 90 74 00
Phone to arrange a visit to the studio of this Sevillian sculptor. The gentle expressions of the Christs and Madonnas he creates for brotherhoods across Spain are enchanting. Manuel Hernandez also sculpts smaller, secular figures out of terracotta, wood and bronze.

**Also:
El Corte Inglés** (F F1)
→ Plaza del Duque de la Victoria, 8

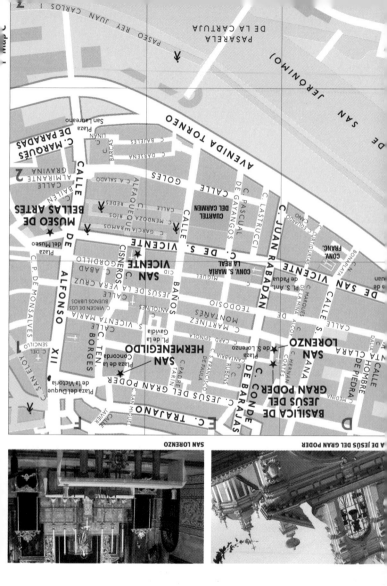

SAN LORENZO

A DE JESÚS DEL GRAN PODER

MONASTERIO DE SANTA MARÍA DE LAS CUEVAS

IDEM

*r), 6–9pm (9.30pm in
r); Fri 7.30am–10pm
–2pm, 5–10pm in
r); Sun 8am–2pm,
(9.30pm in summer)
century Gothic-
ar church, altered
en the 17th and 19th
es. The four chapels
each other in
for: statuary,
d ceilings, baroque
entation. The church-
m has an immense
ece (1623) by
ez Montañez.

**vento de
lemente** (F C1)
eposo, 9
4 37 80 40
y appointment

11am–noon, 4.30–5.30pm
This was the first convent
of nuns to be founded
in Seville after it was
reconquered by Ferdinand
III in 1248. Only the single-
nave church (18th century)
is open to the public. It
houses works by Francisco
Pacheco (*retablo de San
Juan Bautista*), Valdés Leal
(*St Ferdinand entering
Seville*), Felipe de Rivas and
Lucas Valdés (*Retablo
Mayor*, 1639–1747).

★ **Puente
de la Barqueta** (F B1)
A single white arch, slender
lines and a series of
cables... Since Expo '92, the
'bridge of the little boat' has

spanned the river between
the city and the island of La
Cartuja, previously linked
by boat.

★ **Isla Mágica** (F A2)
→ *Isla de la Cartuja*
Tel. 902 16 17 16
Times vary, call beforehand
A discovery park since 1997
on the site of Expo '92.
Find out what it was like to
discover America – and
have fun at the same time.

★ **Monasterio de
Santa María de
las Cuevas** (F D3)
→ *Isla de la Cartuja*
Tel. 955 03 70 70
*Tue-Fri 10am–9pm; Sat
11am–9pm; Sun 11am–3pm*
Christopher Columbus

withdrew to this 15th-
century monastery to
prepare for his second
voyage to the Americas.
In 1841, the Englishman
Charles Pickman installed
a ceramics factory in the
monastery buildings. Since
1998, it has housed the
Andalusian Contemporary
Art Center, creating a
wonderful blend of past
and present and some
striking juxtapositions:
contemporary sculptures
against a cloister backdrop,
factory towers next to an
old bell tower, old stone
alongside fine concrete. It
also holds exhibitions of
contemporary art, of course.

London-Seville via Paris

■ London-Waterloo to Paris-Gare du Nord with Eurostar (15 trains a day)
■ Paris-Austerlitz to Madrid-Atocha: daily, 7.43pm–8.58am
■ Madrid-Atocha to Seville-Santa Justa: with AVE (fast train). Departs every hour (2½hrs).

Eurostar (UK)
→ Tel. 0870 160 66 00
SNCF (France)
→ Tel. 08 36 35 35 35
www.voyages-sncf.com
RENFE (Spanish railways)
→ Tel. 020 7224 0345 (UK)
www.spanish-rail.co.uk
www.renfe.es

ESTACIÓN DE SANTA JUSTA

AEROPUERTO DE SAN PABLO

TUSSAM
→ Av. de Andalucia
Tel. 954 55 72 24
www.tussam.es
Daytime services
→ Daily 6am–11.45pm
■ **Circular routes** (C1-C4)
Circular routes around the city center.
■ **Cross-city routes** (1-2, 5-6) and **radial routes** (10-15, 20-27, 3C 34, 40-43) linking the center with the north, south, east and west of the city.
■ **Terminuses**
Plaza Nueva, plaza de la Encarnación, puente de la Barqueta, Prado de San Sebastiá
Night buses (A1-A6)
→ Sun-Thu midnight–2am; Fri midnight–5am; Sat midnight–6am
Departs every hour fror the Plaza Nueva.
Tickets
On sale at Tussam ticket offices and in kiosks.
→ **Single ticket:**
€1 (from the driver).
→ **Bonobus:**
ten direct journeys (€4.20) or ten journeys with one change, made within the hour (€5.15)
→ **Tarjeta Turistica** (tourist card): 1-day pas (€3), or 3-day pass €7
Tourist bus
Sevilla Tour
→ Tel. 954 50 20 99
www.sevillatour.com
Ticket valid 24 hours.
See Seville from the top of a double-decker bus: from the Torre del Oro, via La Cartuja to the Plaza de España.

---

plenty of character. Five rooms but none with en-suite bathrooms. €40–60.

Hostal Arenal (C C2)
→ C/Pastor y Landero, 21
Tel. 954 22 61 77
Above a local bar and only a stone's throw from the Plaza de Toros. The hotel doesn't have a patio but it does have one very reasonably-priced room (with jacuzzi) which opens onto the roof-terrace (€58). Other rooms €42 .

Hostal San Esteban (B C1)
→ C/San Esteban, 8
Tel. 954 22 25 49
Only a stone's throw from the Casa de Pilatos. The hotel's seven rooms are very cozy. A home from home. €45.

€50–70

Hostal Monreal (A B4)
→ C/Rodrigo Caro, 8
Tel. 954 21 41 66

Hostal Montreal is the ideal hotel if you want to stay in the heart of historic Seville without breaking the bank. Twenty rooms and a terrace with an unrivaled view of La Giralda. The restaurant serves breakfast and lunch only. €50 (with en-suite).

Hostal Toledo (A B3)
→ C/Santa Teresa, 15
Tel. 954 21 53 35
An old townhouse in the Judería (Jewish quarter) close to the Plaza Santa Cruz. Bright, attractively proportioned rooms. €50.

Hotel Europa (A A6)
→ C/Jimios, 5
Tel. 954 21 43 05
www.hoteleuropasevilla.com
A simple hotel, but with all mod cons, near the cathedral. Some of the 16 spacious rooms are decorated with ceramic tiles. €54–90.

Hostal Atenas (B C2)
→ C/Caballerizas, 1
Tel. 954 21 80 47

www.hostal-atenas.com
A typical Sevillian house with a light, beautiful inner lobby area filled with plants. Very clean, simple rooms with en-suite bathrooms and air conditioning. €59.

Hotel Sevilla (E E4)
→ C/Daóiz, 5
Tel. 954 38 41 61
www.hotel-sevilla.com
This hotel near the Alameda de Hércules is ideal if you want to be off the main tourist routes but near the center. There are 38 rooms, and rooms 31 and 32 have terraces overlooking the pretty Plaza de San Andrés. Air-conditioned rooms. €60.

Hotel Zaida (C B2)
→ C/San Roque, 26
Tel. 954 21 11 38
Experience the pleasures of living in a renovated 18th-century Mudéjar palace, close to the Museo de Bellas Artes. Simple, air-

AIRPORT

Aeropuerto San Pablo
→ Tel. 954 44 90 00
About 4 miles east of
Seville, on the N IV.
For national and
international airlines.
City-center links
Bus Amarillos
→ Tel. 954 98 91 84
Daily 6.15am–11pm
(Mon-Fri every 30 mins,
Sat-Sun every hour).
Duration: 30 mins.
Fare: €2.40.
Stops: Puerta de Jeréz
(opposite the Hotel
Alfonso XIII), Estación
de Santa Justa.
By cab
→ Duration: 15–20 mins.
Fare: €20 (set price).

AIRPORT AND ROAD ACCESS

Except where otherwise
indicated, the prices given
are for a double room with
en-suite bathroom. Some
hotels charge the same
rate whether it is the low
season (temporada baja:
Oct-March) or high season
(temporada alta: April-Sep),
however prices are
doubled and even tripled
(temporada extra) during
the Semana Santa and the
Feria.
Prices given here do not
include the IVA (VAT: 7%).

RENTED
APARTMENTS

Often a more economic
option and the best
way to be 'in the swim'.
There is a minimum stay
of three nights.
Centro Sevilla
Apartamentos
→ C/Adolfo Rodríguez Jurado,
6B (**A** C5)
Tel. 954 50 02 06

www.centrosevilla.com
Twenty or so immaculate
apartments for two to six
people, in or very close
to the city center. TV, air
conditioning. €30/2 pers.
Apartamentos
Murillo (**A** B3)
→ C/Reinoso, 6
Tel. 954 21 09 59
The apartments may be a
bit faded but they are clean
and ideally located in the
heart of the Santa Cruz
district. €94 /1–3 pers.
Patios de Sevilla / Patios
de la Cartuja (**E** C4)
→ Pl/Alameda de
Hércules, 56
Tel. 954 90 49 99
→ C/Lumbreras, 8-10
Tel. 954 90 02 00
Twenty-one and 33
(respectively)
Mediterranean- and Zen-
style hotel-apartments,
overlooking attractive
ocher and vermilion patios
decorated with azulejos.
€77–94 /2 pers.

Less than €60

Hostal Paco's (C B2)
→ C/Pedro del Toro, 7
Tel. 954 21 71 83
The 13 small rooms are
modest but clean and tidy.
€ 35.
Pensión Alcázar (A C4)
→ C/Dean Miranda, 12
Tel. 954 22 84 57
A small boarding house
next to the Alcázar. Three
of the 8 rooms open onto
a terrace where you can
enjoy a drink and a view
of La Giralda. €35–48.
Pensión Vergara (A B3)
→ C/Ximénez de Enciso, 11
Tel. 954 21 56 68
A 15th-century townhouse
with tastefully decorated,
spacious rooms. Its charm
makes up for the lack of en-
suite facilities. €40.
Hotel Romero (C B2)
→ C/Gravina, 21
Tel. 954 21 13 53
Choose between the first-
floor rooms, which are

en-suite, and the brig
more attractive secon
floor rooms with share
facilities. €40.
Hostal Roma (C B2)
→ C/Gravina, 34
Tel. 954 50 13 00
This Andalusian-style
hotel, with its patio an
blue and copper-color
azulejos, opened in 20
with 17 modern, pleas
rooms. €40–45.
Hostal
Guadalquivir (C D4)
→ C/Pagés del Corro, 5
Tel. 954 33 21 00
One of the few inexpe
hotels in the Triana di
near the Plaza del
Altozano. Friendly we
and a pleasant little T
room. Rooms vary in
standard, so ask to se
them first. €40–60.
**Conception Velázqu
Hidalgo (F** E1)
→ C/Martínez Montañé
Tel. 954 90 21 43
A charming house wit

Transportation and hotels in Seville

Circular routes
Privately-run routes
Cross-city routes
Sat & bank hols only
5 Terminus
21 Line number

MIRAFLORES
GIRALDA NORTE
ZODIACO
ESTACIÓN DE SANTA JUSTA
SAN CARLOS

← CEMENTERIO DE SAN FERNANDO

BARZOLA

LA MACARENA

HOSPITAL DE LAS CINCO LLAGAS
BASÍLICA DE LA MACARENA
SAN LUIS
SANTA CATALINA

CALLE FERIA

Pl. de la Encarnación

Alameda de Hércules

PAL. DE LEBRIJA

CONV. DE S. CLEMENTE
SAN LORENZO
Pl. del Duque de la Victoria

SAN VICENTE

ISLA MÁGICA
RÍO GUADALQUIVIR
MUSEO DE BELLAS ARTES

PARQUE JARDÍN DEL GUADALQUIVIR

(saturdays & bank hols)

LA CARTUJA

MONASTERIO DE SANTA MARÍA DE LAS CUEVAS

HUERTA
S. TERESA

NERVIÓN

EL PLANTINAR

HUERTA
DEL PILAR

LA CALZADA

SAN BERNARDO

HUERTA
DE LA SALUD

EL PORVENIR

CASA
DE PILATOS

SANTA
CRUZ

Pl. Don Juan
de Austria

PLAZA
DE ESPAÑA

MUSEO DE ARTES Y
COSTUMBRES
POPULARES

MUSEO
ARQUEOLÓGICO

PARQUE DE
MARÍA LUISA

CENTRO

REAL
ALCÁZAR

UNIVERSIDAD

GIRALDA

CATEDRAL

PAL. DE
S. TELMO

AYUNTAMIENTO

Puerta
de Jeréz

Plaza
Nueva

21 23 25
26 30 31
33 34

EL
ARENAL

TORRE
DEL ORO

XIII)

LOS
REMEDIOS

PLAZA DE TOROS
DE LA MAESTRANZA

FERIA
DE ABRIL

TRIANA

(CANAL DE ALFONSO

(C

NUESTRA
SEÑORA DE LA O

PARQUE
DE LOS
PRÍNCIPES

EL LEÓN

EL TARDÓN

cious, luxurious rooms.
5–290.
**el las Casas de la
ería (A** A2)
/Dos Hermanas, 7
54 41 51 50
.casasypalacios.com
dream hotel occupies
e mansions in the
ría (Jewish quarter).
8 luxury rooms
ook a maze of
c patios with lush
tation, mosaics and
tains. Bearing in mind
the place offers, it is
ively inexpensive and
ively sublime.
–180.
**l Las Casas
Rey de Baeza (B** B1)
*Santiago (plaza Jesús de
dención, 2)*
54 56 14 96
hospes.es
otel in a the heart of
tional Seville is
ious with simplicity.
design, natural
rials and light colors

are the order of the day.
Rooms are arranged over
two floors around a pretty
interior courtyard. All are
very soberly decorated in
cream hues, with stone
floors, marble and wood in
the bathrooms, stereo,
DVD players, shower with
hydromassage. Dream pool
on the terrace. €149–185.

**Hotel Casa
Imperial (B** B2)
→ *C/Imperial, 29*
Tel. 954 50 03 00
www.casaimperial.com
This superb historic
townhouse, the former
residence of the major-
domo to the marquis of the
Casa de Pilatos, was once
linked to the *casa*
by an underground tunnel.
The 25 small apartments
combine classic design
with rustic elements that
add a touch of rural charm
to this urban residence.
A hotel with class.
€200–250.

More than €215

Hotel Melia Colón (C B2)
→ *C/Canalejas, 1*
Tel. 954 50 55 99
www.solmelia.com
This hotel (218 rooms)
is an institution, as it
is where the *toreros*
don their costumes
before the *corrida*.
Soak up the atmosphere
at the El Burladero
restaurant or at the café-
bar, Tasca del Burladero.
From €310.

Hotel Alfonso XIII (D A3)
→ *C/San Fernando, 2*
Tel. 954 91 70 00
www.westin.com/alfonsoxiii
A magnificent neo-Mudéjar
monument and *the* luxury
hotel in Seville. In 1995,
it welcomed the royal
families invited to the
wedding of the Infanta
Elena. It has 147 rooms
and 19 sumptuous suites.
Glamorous throughout.
From €466.

BY CAB

Official cabs are white
with a yellow stripe
decorated with the
city's coat of arms.
Fares
Pick-up charge: €1.10.
Minimum charge: €2.85.
Surcharge (25%) 10pm–
6am and public
holidays.
Reservations

Radio-Taxis
→ *Tel. 954 58 00 00*
Radio-Taxis Giralda
→ *Tel. 954 67 55 55*
TeleTaxis
→ *Tel. 954 62 22 22*

BY CAR

Car rental
There are a number of
car-rental agencies at the
San Pablo airport and
Santa Justa train station.
Drivers must be over 21
and have held a driving
licence for at least one
year.
Speed limits
30 mph in built-up
areas; 55 mph outside
built-up areas;
75 mph on freeways.
Parking
Parking is difficult in the
narrow streets of Seville.
Parking lots
→ *Pl. de la Concordia,
pl. de la Encarnación,
pl. San Pedro,
C/Marqués de Paradas*

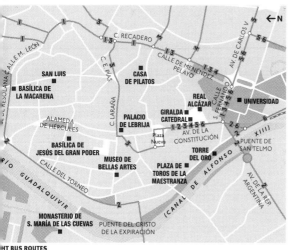

Map labels (within image): C. RECADERO, C. E. PIAS, CALLE DE MENENDEZ PELAYO, AV. DE CARLOS V, SAN LUIS, CASA DE PILATOS, BASÍLICA DE LA MACARENA, C. E. PIAS, REAL ALCÁZAR, UNIVERSIDAD, ALAMEDA DE HÉRCULES, PALACIO DE LEBRIJA, GIRALDA CATEDRAL, C. LARAÑA, BASÍLICA DE JESÚS DEL GRAN PODER, AV. DE LA CONSTITUCIÓN, Plaza Nuevo, MUSEO DE BELLAS ARTES, TORRE DEL ORO, PUENTE DE SAN TELMO, CALLE DEL TORNEO, PLAZA DE TOROS DE LA MAESTRANZA, CANAL DE ALFONSO, AV. DE LA REP. ARGENTINA, RÍO GUADALQUIVIR, MONASTERIO DE S. MARÍA DE LAS CUEVAS, PUENTE DEL CRISTO DE LA EXPIRACIÓN

←N

NIGHT BUS ROUTES

COACH STATIONS

Plaza de Armas
→ Tel. 954 90 77 37
Buses to Spain's main
cities and some regional
destinations including
Itálica and Huelva
→ *Itálica: daily 7am–10pm
(Mon-Sat every 30 mins,
Sun every hour)*
→ *Huelva: daily 7.30am–
9.30am (every hour)*
**Prado de San
Sebastián**
→ Tel. 954 41 71 11
Across Andalusia
including Écija, Osuna,
Carmona and Cádiz
*Daily 7am–10/10.30pm
(Mon-Fri every 30 mins,
Sat-Sun every hour). Cádiz
approx. every 2 hours*

BY B

---

ditioned, rooms, with
mod cons. Some even
re a private balcony
king onto the quiet
eet. Truly pleasant. €60.
stal Goya (A A4)
→ C/Mateos Gago, 31
954 21 11 70
w.hostalgoyasevilla.com
enty rooms decorated
irely in white in a quiet
nhouse opposite the
rch of Santa Cruz. €60.
stal Van Gogh (A C5)
→ C/Miguel Mañara, 1
954 56 37 27
intastic use of warm
ors in all its rooms pays
nage to the hotel's
mesake. All of the 14
rooms are different.
8.
stal Sierpes (B D3)
→ C/Corral del Rey, 22
954 22 49 48
w.hsierpes.com
out 150 yards from La
alda, this hotel really
es value for money.
vely vestibule with

lace hangings and 36 light,
airy, air-conditioned rooms
around a charming patio.
Small traditional bar next
door. Parking. €68.

€70–145

Hotel Plaza Sevilla (C B2)
→ C/Canalejas, 2
Tel. 954 21 71 49
www.hotelplazasevilla.com
A hotel housed in a fine
building by Aníbal
González and well situated
at the end of a busy
shopping street (C/San
Eloy). The 1950s rooms
are rather old-fashioned –
try to get one with a
balcony. Elevator, laundry
room, air conditioning and
parking nearby. €70.
**Hotel Amadeus
Sevilla (A** A3)
→ C/Farnesio, 6
Tel. 954 50 14 43
www.hotelamadeus
sevilla.com
A hotel for lovers of music

and Mozart. Each of the
14 rooms are decorated
differently and sound-
proofed as some of them
even have their own
piano. The hotel welcomes
artists and performers for
exhibitions and concerts.
€80–95.
**Hotel Plaza
de Armas (C** B3)
→ Av. Marqués de Paradas
Tel. 954 90 19 92
www.nh-hoteles.es
This ultramodern hotel
(475 standard rooms)
overlooking the
Guadalquivir was built
for Expo '92. Superb
solarium with wooden
slatting and a panoramic
pool. €99–140.
Hotel San Gil (E B3)
→ C/Parras, 28
Tel. 954 90 68 11
www.fp-heteles.com
Magnificent townhouse
built in 1901 and renovated
in 2000. The 61 rooms are
bright and stylish. There's

also a small garden,
superb rooftop solarium
and pool with a view of
La Macarena. €101–155.
**Hotel Las Casas de
los Mercaderes (B** D5)
→ C/Álvarez Quintero, 9-13
Tel. 954 22 58 58
www.casasypalacios.com
A hotel two steps away
from the Plaza Nueva, with
a patio that dates back to
the 18th century. All 47
rooms are spacious, well
equipped and tastefully
furnished. €112–135.

€145–215

Hotel Los Seises (A A4)
→ C/Segovias, 6
Tel. 954 22 94 95
www.hotellosseises.com
This luxury hotel occupies
part of the buildings of
the Palacio Arzobispal.
It boasts a wonderful
pool with a view of the
cathedral and a dining
room above Roman ruins!

Spa
€2
**Hot
Jud**
→ C
Tel.
ww
This
thre
Jude
Its x
ove
idyl
veg
fou
wha
rela
pos
€1
**Hot
del**
→ C
la Re
Tel.
ww
This
trad
luxu
Here
mat

Street names, monuments and places to visit are listed alphabetically. They are followed by a map reference, of which the initial letter(s) in bold (**A**, **B**, **C**...) relate to the matching map(s) within this guide.